COME PASSION

THE SOULFUL ART OF HEALING TRAUMA

COLLEEN E. CLARK, MSW, RCSW

Come Passion

Second Print Edition
ISBN: 978-3-98832-310-1
Published by Vine Leaves Press 2026

Previously published by Ingenium Books Publishing Inc.
Print ISBN: 978-1-990688-15-7
Electronic ISBN: 978-1-990688-16-4

Cover design by Jessica Bell

COME PASSION

THE SOULFUL ART OF HEALING TRAUMA

COLLEEN E. CLARK, MSW, RCSW

Come Passion

Second Print Edition
ISBN: 978-3-98832-310-1
Published by Vine Leaves Press 2026

Previously published by Ingenium Books Publishing Inc.
Print ISBN: 978-1-990688-15-7
Electronic ISBN: 978-1-990688-16-4

Cover design by Jessica Bell

PRAISE FOR COLLEEN E. CLARK, MSW, RCSW

In *Come Passion: The Soulful Art of Healing Trauma*, Colleen Clark provides a comprehensive yet readily interpretable description of the challenges in effectively treating complex psychological trauma. This overview serves as an initial roadmap, which is then paired with a truly innovative approach to the foundational elements in "preparing" each client for optimal treatment results with Accelerated Resolution Therapy (ART). Whereas most psychotherapies (including ART) are manualized, or procedure-based (e.g., analogous to a medical intervention, such as surgery), Colleen's approach more closely parallels personalized medicine. Thus, it is no surprise as to the singular positive impact she has had in training hundreds of clinicians in ART across Canada, who, in turn, have provided substantial, life-altering relief to thousands of sufferers of psychological trauma. This book is a must read for any clinician interested in seeking a brief yet highly effective approach for treatment of psychological trauma and related comorbidities.

— KEVIN E. KIP, PH.D., FAAAS, FAHA PREVIOUS ART RESEARCHER VICE PRESIDENT OF CLINICAL ANALYTICS, UNIVERSITY OF PITTSBURGH MEDICAL CENTER HEALTH SERVICES DIVISION

At last, an exquisitely written guidebook that provides information on what true trauma therapy is as well as a step-wise approach on how to do it through the lens of ART.

— CAROL GILL, CHIEF PSYCHOLOGIST AT BOWDEN INSTITUTION MENTAL HEALTH DEPARTMENT

The passion and knowledge Colleen has in treating trauma is evident throughout this book. This is a tool every trauma therapist will benefit from having on hand.

— MARNEY RIENDEAU, RN, BSCN, PAST MANAGER OF CALGARY OSI CLINIC, AND LEADER IN PROGRAM DEVELOPMENT IN MENTAL HEALTH

Colleen weaves her knowledge, skills, wisdom and passion to guide us in laying the foundation for practicing Accelerated Resolution Therapy. She invites us to use our heads, hands, hearts in the soul work of helping people find meaningful resolution to their trauma experiences.

— SUZANNE ROSEBRUGH, MSW, RSW, RETIRED CLINICAL SOCIAL WORKER

This thought-provoking book is a valuable resource for any clinician seeking to deepen their therapeutic skills using Accelerated Resolution Therapy (ART). With candour and insight, Colleen Clark draws upon her extensive experience to provide a trauma-informed roadmap that is both practical and enlightening. Through a combination of vivid clinical examples, powerful metaphors, and personal narratives, Clark offers readers a unique perspective on how to implement ART in their own clinical practice.

Self-reflection questions throughout encourage readers to explore their own insights. This approach creates an atmosphere of healing and growth, allowing readers to develop a deeper understanding of themselves and their clients.

Clark's writing is both candid and insightful, and offers readers a rare glimpse into the heart and soul of a master clinician.

— KAITLIN CHIVERS-WILSON, MD, MSC, FRCPC

Colleen Clark was trained by me in Accelerated Resolution Therapy (ART) in 2014. She is a clinical ART specialist who has worked very diligently to bring her passion for ART to Canada and single handedly, with the help of assistants, of course, trained more than 1,000 therapists in this quick and effective modality.

This book offers a comprehensive guide in discussing some of the things that the ART training does not delve deeply into. She offers her view on how to ready a client for ART and shares many of her personal experiences. I consider Colleen to be among my most excellent trainers and look forward to her training many more in ART in the the years to come. Every time she teaches ART to her trainees there are so many more people that will find relief.

— LANEY ROSENZWEIG, MS, LMFT, ART FOUNDER,
CEO ROSENZWEIG CENTER FOR RAPID RECOVERY

With "come passion," Colleen reminds us that psychotherapy isn't about improvising; it's about the value we create when we invest time to get to know our clients, follow our guidelines, and make a lasting difference. Her comprehensive guide follows this path in introducing her unequaled themogram, an undoubtedly optimizing tool. Clinicians will be inspired in reading this manual and profiting from it in their practice.

— NADINE RANCIER, MSW, RSW

WHAT TO DO BEFORE ART

A trauma-informed procedural clinical approach describing the rationale and steps of psycho-education and assessment in the readiness to start delivering Accelerated Resolution Therapy (ART).

We've got this.

This book is not a replacement for professional certification. Whether you have been trained and certified in Accelerated Resolution Therapy (ART) and/or another therapeutic modality, the contents of this book are not intended to override your arrangements with your employer, the ethical contracts you have with the Rosenzweig Center for Rapid Recovery, institutions or agencies, nor is it a legal document that permits you to practice in a way beyond your certification.

This book is not intended to be a substitute for professional medical advice, diagnosis, treatment, for a medical exam or a psychological assessment, nor does it replace the need for services provided by medical professional.

Accelerated Resolution Therapy (ART) is an evidence-based trauma treatment and was granted status from The Substance Abuse and Mental Health Services Administration (SAMHSA) in 2016. SAMHSA was "the agency within the United States Department of Health and Human Services that leads public health efforts to advance the behavioural health of the nation." (https://www.samhsa.gov)

Many of the ideas and recommendations in Come Passion *are mine and mine alone, and do not necessarily reflect those of ART Developer and Founder, Laney Rosenzweig.*

Come Passion: The Soulful ART of Healing Trauma *is written with cultural awareness that includes respect for all First Nations and recognizes that much of the training of ART has taken place, and will take place, on land which is known to be that of the First People's and appropriated under treaty. May the cumulative effect of the therapy that is influenced by the words in this book contribute to reconciliation and healing for all.*

CONTENTS

with my heart and soul
to the absolute loves of my life
my daughters
Cara Elizabeth Semple
and
Bonnie Ann Blasetti

and my precious granddaughter
Sarah Marie Clendon

and
Marley, Maggie, and Callie

and to all who imagine a world John Lennon described

FOREWORD
COMING TO GRACE BEFORE ART

As healers, game-changers, and therapists, there are many ways to bring our gifts to the world, yet we often don't speak of them. Some of our stories may seem so *out there* that we are afraid to share them — but the advancement of humankind, in history and the future, is predicated on the sharing of our stories. Be not afraid. As you age and learn and walk in your calling of healing it makes sense to share... and to know that if what you share doesn't make sense for some, it will for others. In your role as an influencer and inspirer, embrace the sharing of your experience to open the potential of others.

I'll go first.

PERU

I teared up as the plane dipped over the Andes and the little window framed the colonial city of Cusco, Peru. The opportunity to travel to Peru with a group of shamans and travellers had come at an opportune time in my life. I would be on a tour to all the usual places of significance such as Machu Picchu and the Amazon for three weeks. I felt a rush of peaceful purpose and relaxed.

On one of the first nights of the tour, our group took a walk up the side of the mountain — a narrow, precarious path. Had I been a star looking down at us, I'd have described it as a procession as we inclined our way, back and forth, to the top. Along the way, we met Andean women dressed in cascading layers of colourful clothing: embroidered skirts, capes, shawls, and hats like baskets atop their heads. Flute players played. Feet padded surefootedly. Lungs savoured precious breaths as hearts recalibrated to the higher altitude. Myths inside me called out, "Careful, not too close to the sun." And a billowing calm answered: "It's okay, there is nothing to fear, for the moon is the gatekeeper."

We continued to travel the path, and there were moments when a few members of our group stumbled. We took a detour into a cave — one of my life fears, but I survived. — And then we were on top of the mountain, on a plateau, under the velvet night sky. Silent. Contemplative. Grateful. Amazed. Suddenly, one individual began to sing "Amazing Grace."

After time had stood still for who knows how long, we began our descent. Partway down, a little boy, probably about eight, handed me a magnetic rock. He looked into my eyes and said, "You are a healer." I accepted the stone — a jewel from a sacred messenger.

I would have thought this a dream had I not been holding the stone the next morning when I woke. Later that day as I sat on the bus returning from Machu Pichu, a fellow traveller jostling next to me as we bumped up and down, I remembered my dream from the night before.

"I had a dream last night," I said to him. "I'm supposed to get a drum."

"Well," the traveller said mysteriously, "we will get off the bus here. I know someone who has a drum for you."

And with that, he told the driver to stop, and we stepped onto the dusty road.

From when I was a child, I'd been able to see energy and how energy could help me create harmony and peace. So, here in Peru, this wasn't my first rodeo with a spiritual experience. I already believed that our whole lives are a spiritual experience. But this was different. Shimmering. Profound.

The shaman-traveller seatmate took me into a shop filled with shaman stuff and, on the floor, was a baby who would, I was told, become a shaman too. As I stepped to a specific spot, by the counter, I saw the drum from my dream. "That's it," I said. "That's the drum in my dream last night. That's the drum I am to have."

The shop owner approached. "That's my drum," he said. "See how it hangs here by the counter with my other things?"

"I was told in a dream I was to have it," I said.

He took the drum down. "A double-sided, sacred heart-beat llama drum," he explained, and then began to beat it, slowly, rhythmically, staring into my eyes. Past my eyes. Into my soul. He stopped beating, still staring into me.

"You are a healer," he said. "You need to take this with you." And he handed me the drum.

And I did take it with me. I used this drum back home in Canada to help people as they transitioned from this life to another. It served me, it served us, helping hold space for others at the end of life. And the words of the little boy with the magnetic rock — the rock that was there in the morning but gone once I had the drum — continued to reverberate within me: *You are a healer.*

And I say to you: you are a healer. As you prepare to deliver ART, you will be invited to heal others and to heal yourself.

After the meeting with the boy who told me I was a healer; after the dream where I obtained a drum; after I'd been to the place in the real world where I was given that drum in my dream, the journey took me through another part of Peru — the Amazon. In that sacred space, I stayed ten days with the shamans that accompanied us where we met other shamans who welcomed us to their world.

There we were, at a jungle ecolodge, machetes slicing paths, wild boars, snakes, a paradise of trees. Time spent in narrow dugout boats on the water where magnificent indigo butterflies teased the space between water and air and touched the noses of stacked turtles. The piranhas swam beneath us, occasionally surfacing to feed their own lives and remind us of the trauma.

In the evening there was a ceremony, even though every moment was a sacred service. That evening, I began chanting in a language unfamiliar to the everyday me, but nonetheless familiar in that moment. The shaman explained to me after that it was the Q'eqchi', also spelled and pronounced Kekchi, one of the Mayan languages spoken in parts of Central and South America, including Guatemala and Belize.

How did I know to chant as the indigenous?

Symbolism and the power of our imagination in times where there is great energy is incredible.

And I had another vision. I arrived at the base of another mountain where a panther took me on his back. Around and around we went on a circular path up the mountain until we reached a community of elders. I joined them, and we chanted in Kekchi while the panther waited patiently for me. Then the panther told me it was time to go. Instinctively, I knew I was going to be shown my purpose and, at the same time, profess my purpose to God.

We travelled farther up the mountain until we reached a place resembling a carpenter's shop. I entered. Again, the panther waited.

In this transitional state and place, God was there. I would later open myself to sharing that we each have a God of our own understanding, and, for clarity, I emphasize this too. We each create our own conception of a higher power, a source, that directs our life, our death, our in between, and beyond.

In the carpenter's shop, God gifted me three large bars of gold. "These are going to be your tools," God said. "They are the bricks to change the world."

With the speed of lightning, the symbolism of the three — a trinity — was imprinted on my brain. Later I would think, *ART is three letters, and three is body, mind, and soul.* In the vision-dream, I took the bars with me, joined the panther, and — yes, on his back — we continued to the summit. I dismounted the giant wildcat and carried my bricks of gold, chants resting in my throat, and the panther said, "You no longer need me," and he looked toward a white owl in the distance.

"There's a white owl," I said.

I'd always loved white owls. I had pictures of them in my home. I understood that white owls can travel both worlds.

And the white owl said, "No, you are the white owl."

The vision-dream ended. I spent another five days in the jungle with my fellow travellers: each day unfolding with new clarity.

It was time to return to Calgary and get back to work as a social worker at Calgary Family Services. I tried to put my Peruvian journey into an internal shredder because, really, who would believe me? But I was having trouble making sense of those pages of my story that came from the Amazon and the mountain treks and the shaman and the drum and the panther and the gold bricks and the white owl. What were they all trying to tell me? What was I supposed to do?

Beside the 17th Avenue SE location of Calgary Family Services was a second-hand shop that had been there for years. I'd never been in. But, shortly after my return to work, I found myself standing outside the shop and, in the way that hope intersects with need, I asked the God of my understanding for a sign. *Point me forward,* I asked silently, believing yet not believing an answer would come.

I pushed open the door and entered the store. There, staring down at me from a high shelf was a large ornament: a white owl. *A sign!*

Of course, I purchased it. I still have it. It is perched on my living room mantle and it watches everything.

There is value in looking back at the moments of inspiration that you keep from others because it was too incredible or unusual to believe. Do you create your experiences? Or do they create you? This is one of many questions we ask as we seek to understand our path through life. A path through life that connects our personal life and professional life. We are told that we should keep our professional and personal lives separate — and I advocate boundaries, absolutely — but our values overlap, and our stories and experiences unfold one over the other without recognizing the lines.

Be aware of this. Find your way to bring your story to work every day.

INTRODUCTION

I've been treating patients with trauma-related issues like post-traumatic stress disorder (PTSD) and complex PTSD (C-PTSD) in my private practice and in an Operational Stress Injury (OSI) clinic for a long, long time.

Complex co-morbidity is the norm when therapists interview for PTSD. At the OSI clinic, 80 per cent of the patients with PTSD meet diagnostic criteria for at least one other mental disorder — often some form of depression. Fifty-three per cent of our patients have three or more DSM diagnoses.

As therapists, we struggled to treat these patients. In 2002, Korn and Leeds recommended prolonged stabilization in C-PTSD. Still, many with complex trauma failed to enter remission or were unable to tolerate or benefit from exposure-based treatment.

In 2012 everything changed. At last, there appeared an evidence-based treatment solution. The International Society for Traumatic Stress Studies (ISTSS) released the Expert Consensus Guidelines for Treatment of Complex PTSD in Adults. Highlights included:

- Phase based treatment
- Stabilization and skills building: six months

- Exposure therapy: three to six months
- Symptoms remitting/re-engagement: six to twelve months
- Emphasis of clinician judgment in determining length of each phase
- Importance of clinician and client agreeing on transition to successive phases

In response to the guidelines, we developed a specialized stabilization protocol for use in complex trauma cases in our operational stress injury clinic.

Goals of specialized stabilization for Complex PTSD:

1. Address emotional dysregulation
2. Decrease dissociation
3. Decrease somatic distress
4. Promote identity
5. Address relational disturbance
6. Address spiritual alienation
7. Improve self-development.

Our treatment plans for specialized stabilization were highly individualized and required both a well-trained trauma therapist and committed patient to complete the treatment.

I had been teaching this evidence-based approach for several years and many of our patients were successful in treatment.

The problem was that treatment could take two years or more; this stretched our clinic's resources and of course we were interested in helping our patients recover more quickly so they could gain back quality of life.

The answer to our resource issues and to a more rapid success trajectory for our clients came in the form of Accelerated Resolution Therapy (ART).

I began treating clients of an operational stress injury (OSI) clinic with ART, introducing it as an emerging, brief, exposure-based therapy, in one to five sessions. We conducted psychometric testing and asked patients to self-report on their symptoms: before treatment began, before each session, monthly throughout the treatment, and again at the end. The testing included a forty-five-question outcome questionnaire designed to measure psychotherapy progress in adult clients, and PTSD personal checklists designed for both military and civilian personnel. We also contacted the spouses of our patients to gather their observational feedback about changes in their partner's functioning during and after receiving ART.

The results were dramatic. My patients were reporting a significant decrease in negative symptoms related to their PTSD and other psychological co-morbidities — often as much as 20 to 40 per cent, and all within five to eight treatment sessions. Through narrative reporting, clients and their partners were reporting significant reductions in PTSD symptoms, as well as an overall increase in quality and re-engagement of life. Not only that, but patients moved more quickly through trauma treatment and became engaged in the maintenance and transitional stages of the next stages of treatment. Therefore, clients were reducing their time within the clinic from the average of thirty-three months to attending only eight sessions of ART, then moving on with their lives.

You may a be a doctor with a family practice, a psychiatrist in the military, a psychologist attached to a specific community, or a clinical social worker who serves a prison population. Perhaps you're a counsellor who is part of a team who helps refugees in resettlement, or you are a therapist who travels internationally to serve others in places recovering from natural disasters. You have likely also received training in Accelerated Resolution Therapy (ART). Maybe from me. ART treats the trauma so that the symptoms which arose from that trauma can be seen for what they are — the body's normal responses to trauma — and can then be addressed.

The goal of therapy for a therapist, like you, working the field of trauma, coming from a trauma-informed lens of practice, is to produce an outcome for your clients in which they can talk about the trauma processing in a factual, almost detached way at the completion of the trauma. With Accelerated Resolution Therapy (ART) clients can do this. They will have the facts — and more — at the end of processing.

In delivering ART, you will not experience the same emotional and psychological burden from the witnessing of their stories as other therapies bring to the therapist, thus relieving stress and preventing vicarious traumatization, and in many cases, extending your professional life.

ART has all the requirements and goals in its model to meet the standards of trauma therapy. It unites implicit and explicit memories into a comprehensive narrative of events and aftermath of the traumatic incident. This includes making sense of body sensations and behaviours, and behaviours within that context. It works with the autonomic nervous system (hyper- and hypo-arousal) in connection with those memories. It relegates the traumatic event to the past and allows the client to understand that it was a long time ago, and it is over, and they survived.

Whatever your specialty, or whomever you trained under in ART, you can further improve the outcomes of this therapy by knowing — and practicing — what to do *before* you deliver ART. This is the question I'm asked most frequently in my training rooms. This is the question I answer in this book.

I also offer an advanced session that covers what to do before delivering ART and many of my ART students attend. The reality is that not everyone can manage that and their practice at the same time. If you're one of those therapists, *Come Passion: The Soulful ART of Healing* is for you. It offers insight and guidance to help you grow further, re-energize, and prepare you for successfully delivering ART.

My ART training sessions, and the material you're about to read in *Come Passion*, follow and support ART's protocol, of course. But they're also shaped by my belief that we must bring our whole heart and our whole self into ART. I've long believed that healers understand healing because they have *experienced* healing. And so, you'll find me sharing some of my personal and professional stories to bring context and depth to the nuts and bolts of what to do before delivering ART.

Like many of us in the healing field, I am compelled to leave a legacy. I believe that compassion, self-compassion, and investing in self-care practices are critical for you as a therapist, because they affect your view of yourself as a healer which in turn will affect the outcome of the therapy you deliver.

HOW TO USE THIS BOOK

Come Passion: The Soulful ART of Healing Trauma is more than a manual. It is intended to help you enhance your practice and skills as a trained ART therapist.

In *Section I: Early Days*, I'll share the story of how I came to ART and provide a bit of a refresher on ART: what it is, what's involved in the training, and where and who is requesting ART training support.

Section II: You, the Therapist is where we review foundational elements that are critical to supporting your ART work. We revisit trauma, the biology of the brain, and talk about attachment, development, and avoidance. We dig into cultural competence and specialized population. And then, because as a therapist working with trauma clients you're exposed to vicarious trauma, there's a whole chapter dedicated to self-care.

The rubber hits the road in *Section III: You and Your Client before ART.* This is where you'll find the action steps laid out that answer the question, "What do I do before ART?" I'll walk you through how to establish a positive relationship, provide psycho-education, conduct a thorough assessment, develop themes, and explain ART.

And then in *Section IV: The Future with ART*, we check in on where we are going in a world that needs more ART. And I've also included helpful documents in the *Resources* section at the end.

Each chapter ends with space for you to record thoughts and notes directly in this book, and several chapters, in particular those in *Section III: You and Your Client before ART*, pose questions for you to answer — which, again, you can write in this book. There's also room for you to make other reflective notes. My intention is that this becomes your book and you keep it, evolve it, and refer to it often as you become more adept at delivering ART to heal your clients of their trauma.

It's important for me to clarify for you that while I provide several anecdotal stories from real client experiences, I have changed details and ensured that privacy and confidentiality is respected at all times. Similarities between these examples, stories, or anecdotes and any person, alive or dead, is strictly coincidental.

The way to use this book is to participate in its construction and to customize it for yourself. Can you *imagine* what it would be like to get together with other practitioners and share the notes you've made so that the way of delivering ART further evolves?

As human beings, we all have the capacity and ability to cope and survive through our own unique experiences until, in some cases, a long-closed door — behind which is a traumatic event, or more than one — opens, and our world is turned upside down. Terror, fear, confusion, desperation, powerlessness, and even thoughts of suicide can send us into crisis.

The human spirit seeks to live but, to heal, the depths of remembering, regaining understanding, and integration of self needs to occur. It is not easy to embark on this journey as the outcome is unknown. People just know they cannot live this way anymore.

Why we suffer, and the degree to which we suffer, are sometimes impossible to fathom, but we can heal in this lifetime, continually growing, developing, and evolving.

The sun and the moon tell the time, dividing days, months, and seasons; our lives exist inside an exquisite timepiece. When something amazing happens we'll say, "We were in the right place at the right time."

Timing impacts the *when* of a therapeutic relationship. So does the metaphorical *where*. Excellent therapists meet clients where they are at. A place on the path of life where clients get to hear how they have done all the right things to survive, and that their coping skills kicked in to save their life. They learn how symptoms developed out of the body knowing what it had to do to damage-control the trauma. It is then that clients experience the paradigm shift that is ART.

No matter what you know, there is always more you can learn and, conversely, teach and share with others. The depth of your knowledge and comfort with the above will profoundly impact the success of your ART sessions. As you know, the symptoms are often gone or lessened due to ART.

You know that there is a powerful attunement component — the reactiveness we have to another person — in ART. The bond between you and your client will form quickly because of the short timeline to relief. You'll bear witness to their stories and help to reshape, rewrite, edit, and add chapters to them. You'll remind clients that they are the heroes of their own story. The role you fill as supporter, facilitator, and clinical therapist is akin to holding space for them and saying, "I know, it's like you're in a dark tunnel. I am with you in that tunnel, and I assure you I see the light at the end of it."

The more thoroughly you fulfill your duties — by knowing what to do before delivering ART — the greater your contribution to the healing the world needs.

Let's begin.

SECTION 1: EARLY DAYS

CHAPTER 1
HOW I CAME TO ART

Serving others has been a part of my life for as long as I can remember. As a clinical social worker and clinical supervisor with the Alberta College of Social Workers (ACSW), my life has comprised one journey inside another inside another until I reached a level that merged the science I'd learned with my soul's purpose.

When I was three years old, I stood on my street in Edmonton looking up at the clouds in the blue sky. I asked where I came from, and *how* I should do what I already knew I was meant to do. I'd been adopted and was already reaching out for explanations beyond the legal human ties.

When I was thirty-seven and found my family of birth, the experience was so profound that I changed my master's project and called it "Coming Home to Self." I travelled to New York and presented at two conferences about this work. One of the conferences was at the Roosevelt Hotel in NYC, where I was approached by a fellow adoptee. I asked them what they knew of their birth and adoption story. "I know where I was found," they said. We jumped in a cab and they gave the driver the address. When we got there, the building was long gone but there were big guardian-like trees. I suggested we walk together among the trees as this was where their mother had last connected with them. We sat on a beautiful bench while they let the trees witness the mingling of their mother's energy with their own. "Now you can come here anytime," I said.

The foundling wrote to me later, explaining that they had always struggled to connect with others. Now that they'd "come home," connection was no longer an issue.

My conference presentations led to an invitation from the Province of Alberta to set up a search agency for adoptees. My model offered a therapeutic opportunity and was used as a way to help searchers and finders and birth families to heal. At one point I even drove an adoptee to another province to meet their ninety-year-old birthmother.

In my career, I'd end up taking several paths, all within the field of healing. Every role was associated with those who had experienced trauma... even my own. This all contributed to understanding how to work with others through a trauma-informed lens.

In February 2014, I was preparing for what felt like my first vacation ever; the brutal Canadian winter punishing even those who love winter sports. I was working as a trauma therapist at an operational stress injury clinic (OSI) in Calgary, Alberta, one of several clinics in Canada where assessments are provided to first responders (all organizations and sectors) who are experiencing PTSD and their families. It was my dream job — at that time the highlight of the previous thirty years as a clinical social worker and trauma therapist. I was also preparing for the role of a sessional for the Faculty of Social Work at the University of Calgary where I'd be, for the first time, creating and teaching the mental health and trauma course. The textbook was ordered, and I was excited to start preparing for the course during my (ahem) time off in Florida.

Two days prior to my departure, an opportunity arrived in my email inbox — and I knew my world was about to change.

The email was from the OSI's clinical director, psychiatrist Dr. Stephen Boucher, who was forwarding an article describing the latest research on a new and promising evidence-informed trauma treatment called Accelerated Resolution Therapy.

Sure, I was leaving in two days but, always curious, I read the article. And my excitement grew as I noted the authors' names: Dr. Kevin Kip from the University of South Florida and Laney Rosenzweig, founder and CEO of the Rosenzweig Rapid Recovery Center (RRRC). I Googled "Accelerated Resolution Therapy" and discovered there was a basic training. In Florida. During the time I would be there. And close to where I was going to be staying.

Timing is everything.

At lunchtime, I spoke about the article with the rest of the clinical team, and asked another colleague, a psychiatrist, if they would review the research and give me his opinion. We already used evidence-based treatments at the clinic, including EMDR and Prolonged Exposure. The non-biased review of ART from this psychiatrist was positive, hopeful, and promising. I secured the support of my manager to take my vacation time, paid for and attended the training in Florida.

There were nine of us in the basic training in Tampa, Florida. I was the only Canadian. I met and immediately formed a strong connection to the visionary, founder, and CEO of the ART organization, Laney Rosenzweig, who had developed ART the program in 2008. More than 300 therapists in the US had so far been trained in ART.

It was as if my life had been divinely choreographed to include ART. The theory and foundations of the model, including the use of bi-lateral stimulations, fit seamlessly on top of the eye movement desensitization and reprocessing (EMDR) training I'd taken in New York in 1992 from EMDR originator Dr. Francine Shapiro. At that time, EMDR was my trauma therapy of choice.

During that initial training, Laney Rosenzweig said three things about ART that struck me like a lightning bolt and have stuck with me ever since:

"trust the eye movements," "less gab more grab," "when in doubt, process out."

When the training sessions were done, Rosenzweig and I shared dinner and talked about the future of ART. My experience in the training had me creating and imagining possibilities for the clients I served at an OSI clinic, those I treated in my private practice, and the university students I would soon teach.

I told Laney I wanted to introduce ART to practitioners and their clients in Canada. Laney was supportive and open to it. When I returned to Canada, I ran a pilot project, with the support of my manager, for twenty-three of my clients with PTSD — complex, Type 1, and Type 2 — who had limited success with other therapies. Within eight sessions, there were positive changes. Their trauma therapy was complete.

I didn't realize it then, but the seeds for this book were sown. In delivering that pilot project, I learned what I and other therapists needed to do before delivering ART, and so began my work developing the platform that you're reading about in this book. I also presented the outcomes of the pilot project at the Canadian Institute for Military and Veteran Health Research (CIMVHR). Dr. Kevin Kip attended and spoke more about the therapy. My findings became part of the literature at the institute.

Laney Rosenzweig traveled to Canada and trained the rest of our OSI therapy team. ART became the therapy of choice for our clients and clinicians.

I returned to the US and became trained in Advanced and Enhanced ART. Later I was asked to go back to become one of five ART trainers, which included the renowned Dr. Charles Hoge, Walter Reed's head psychiatrist. Again, I was the only Canadian.

I drank in all the training. The healer in me knew that this represented incredible steps forward in therapy. I completed the trainings, dreamed my dream, then set about making it a reality.

Thank you, cold winter for pointing me south.

In the train-the-trainer program in Tampa, we discussed what it is to be a humanitarian; someone who is concerned with or seeking to promote

human welfare and improve the happiness of people. A compassionate human being. The first obligation is to do no harm.

We discussed how the most powerful people are not the most assertive or self-interested, but those who have done the most to promote humanitarianism around the world. Our discussion revolved around how planning for the future success of others, therefore the world, means having *imagination*, and wisdom. We batted words around that brought more energy to the group: inspired, imaginative, creative, inventive, ingenious, enterprising, innovative, insightful, perceptive, intuitive, prescient, discerning, wise, clever, resourceful, idealistic, and quixotic.

Compassion and *imagine* had long been words which resonated for me. The more I heard the former, the more I said it, and the more I practiced it, it became: *come, passion*. With the latter word, imagine, John Lennon's ideals and lyrics lapped waves against my soul, and connected with my passion.

When we imagine, we evoke the visionary in one another. This is what I believe, but it is also what happened to me just before, during, and after the ART training.

These initial results at our Canadian clinic in Calgary appeared to support the recent experience and empirical data from the multiple studies conducted in the US, through the University of South Florida with Dr. Kevin Kip and his team, who were studying utilizing ART within military and civilian populations.

I soon found that I was being referred clients who were identified as being treatment resistant due to their projected length of treatment and complexity of their PTSD.

Dr. Kevin Kip and I presented at the national conference of the CIMVR in Toronto in November 2014. Our focus was to share ART's international research and the initial Canadian findings. Dr. Kip would handle the former, and I'd handle the latter using the treatment experience and results of using ART in Calgary.

The expansion of ART in Canada continued. I became the trainer for Canada in 2015.

THE PARADIGM SHIFT

We continued to deliver ART. The more we delivered, the more patients began requesting it as a first line treatment.

As I delivered ART and trained others to use it in their clinical practices, I came to understand that, just as in my career in social work had emphasized, delivery of therapy may be an integral part of healing, but that healing could be even more successful if I invested in helping other ART trainees understanding what to do before providing ART to inform, energize, and essentially enhance the therapy.

Because of my call to heal, I've become a part of the solution of helping myriad first-responder professions — where the dynamics of the job demand a participation which raises the incidence of traumatic stress — address the issues of complex trauma. So successful are the outcomes with all ages and traumas that there are already new relationships with several agencies and organizations for which ART is being disseminated across Canada: military bases, police departments, correctional centres including the Bowden Institution in Alberta. Additionally, international connections, to places where crises have and are occurring, continue to form.

ART has recently been reviewed by indigenous leaders and a pilot project initiated. At the time of this writing, training is in place for First Nations' therapists. This is a momentous and progressive step for Canada; it will contribute to the reconciliation process.

At the time of this writing, the Canadian military is engaged in an intensive study to involve ART. Studies within first responder groups will continue to be initiated.

Perhaps over the next decade, ART will become synonymous with healing trauma, and you will be a part of that breakthrough whereby the world expands trauma-informed care in ways we cannot currently envision.

For now, know that healers like you — who deal with traumatized humans — need ART because it is less intensive than other modalities by way of its direct route to handling the trauma. In your duty to facilitate the steps of ART — including knowing what to do before you deliver ART -

see yourself as a choreographer of healing and relief for the client. As the client works on the right side of the brain and the subconscious, the trauma will be replaced with positive images and the body will be reset.

As of 2023, there are just four other clinical ART specialists with the highest level of certification who can train beyond Enhanced and Advanced, and serve as experts in presentations and discussions about ART. I have trained over one-thousand therapists in Canada and internationally. Perhaps I've trained you.

If I look at what drew me to ART, before I was trained and began training others, I have to return full circle to the person who first brought ART to my attention. Dr. Stephen Boucher's inner sense prompted him to forward that initial email about ART to me. He has since been more than a driving force in supporting my pursuit of ART — his dedication and passion to the subject of healing as real as his friendship has been loyal. As I was finalizing this book, Dr. Boucher... Stephen... continued to encourage and support its completion. What brought me to ART was the heart (heART) of a gentle, caring friend and colleague and a remarkable professional.

QUESTIONS

What does your path to ART look like?

REFLECTIVE NOTES

CHAPTER 2
REFRESHER ON ART

You know about ART already or you wouldn't be reading this book. I still want to provide a baseline summary of the therapy because it provides a foundation for you as we prepare for the description of the steps of what to do before you deliver ART.

ART treatment protocols are directive, procedural, standardized, and easy to apply to a range of diagnoses. It's evidence-based exposure-based psychotherapy that processes body memory-somatic, uses symbolic imagery and aims to replace negative images rather than desensitize or reframe the experience, involves re-scripting of trauma memories. It doesn't take as long as conventional evidence-based therapies like EMDR or Prolonged Exposure. ART is not hypnotherapy, requires no homework on the part of the patient, has higher completion rates than other trauma therapies, and a low rate of side effects. The ART therapist and patient will identify themes, then a scene to process in a sixty-minute session. The procedure, which has a beginning, middle, and end, is structured, safe, and creative. The patient will always have the facts, their emotional distress will be decreased, and their trauma processed into long term memory. The amygdala will be reset to be responsive versus reactive.

ART has proven effective for PTSD (single incident, multiple, and childhood traumas), depression, anxiety, phobia, obsessive compulsive disorder, addictions, and myriad other issues. The patient does not have to tell their story (again) to move through the therapy, yet they will complete a cohesive narrative at the end of the sessions. Because the client doesn't tell their trauma story, the ART therapist doesn't have to listen to their trauma story, which protects them from vicarious traumatization.

Even though the overall anticipated time with them will be shorter than with traditional trauma therapies, a bond — attunement — between patient and therapist will form quickly — in part because the ART therapist is attuned to them, in part because they'll experience relief much sooner than with traditional therapy. This relief is relief from the trauma — so that the symptoms can be dealt with once the root of the trauma has been addressed.

It is in dealing with the symptoms, later, that they may have longer term relationships such as with AA, NA, or a sleep clinic, for example.

ABOUT ART TRAINING

In Canada, mental health therapists now trained in ART in Canada include psychiatrists, clinical social workers, clinical nurse specialists, psychologists, and occupational therapists. Some work in private practice, others work in provincially or federally funded centres across Canada.

There are three levels of training in ART:

1. Basic ART Training (three days). Basic ART training demonstrates application of the therapy model and involves two practicums and several interactive lectures. We discuss the power of the eye movements in addition to a foundational review of several evidenced based therapies. We discuss how these therapies, combined with ART's creative therapeutic interventions result in effectiveness of ART to treat a multitude of problems. Participants learn how to use ART with clients to reduce the symptoms of anxiety, sexual abuse, grief, obsessive compulsive thinking, PTSD, etcetera. This process accelerates

resolution of problems as it facilitates the client in making cognitive and behavioural changes.

2. Advanced Training (two days). Must have completed Basic Training plus thirty documented sessions of ART, and complete Advanced Training within one year of completing Basic. Participants learn how to use metaphors as a stand-alone intervention, which allows the reader or listener to picture things, to understand, and relate to their own situation (ART's metaphorical moment), and learn advanced interventions.
3. Enhanced Training (two days). Must have completed both Basic and Advanced Training. Participants focus on specialized problems like Obsessive-compulsive Disorder, substance abuse, and phobias. They engage in case consultations and delve deeper into the use of specialized ART interventions.

Registration requirements for ART training:

- Must be a licensed mental health professional or RN with psychiatric training
- Must provide a copy of a valid license
- Must provide field of practice/speciality and length of time in practice
- Must sign non-disclosure

Upon completion of ART training, participants receive:

1. Certificate of attendance
2. Option to audit additional Basic Training sessions for one year at no cost

Participants can also join IS-ART, the International Society of Accelerated Resolution Therapy.

ART STORIES OF HEALING

I'm sharing my (abbreviated) notes from one specific client, details changed for confidentiality purposes, following completion of our ART therapy together.

1. Reduced stabilization period
2. Trauma treatment successful with noted rapid decrease in PTSD symptoms (including emotional numbing) as reported by patient and significant partner
3. Average of five to seven sessions of ART
4. Therapeutic gains were maintained in follow-up (post-traumatic growth)
5. Clients able to actively participate in skill building maintenance and transition phase of treatment
6. Clients have lessened time in treatment
7. Increased quality of life
8. Return to employment and school.

But the overviews and stories show more than the lists. And the first-hand accounts from clients are powerful. (Again, note that while the client stories or examples I share are based on real clients and real therapy, I have changed details in order to maintain confidentiality.)

Combat Veteran

Some years ago, I worked with a combat veteran who had returned from war and coped with their trauma by immersing themselves in even more work. They'd been labeled a workaholic. Then they began to drink alcohol. Never once had they disclosed the nature of their combat experiences to their family members. The family saw the person as cranky and hardworking, simply a product of their generation. When they became hospitalized after an injury, family and caregivers became concerned the ex-member was developing dementia. But some bright professionals believed that they had actually activated PTSD.

This person came to see me. For the first time in their life, they were able to tell their story. The outcomes for them and their family were manyfold: their nightmares ceased and they came to a place of peace and so did their family. That's the goal for everyone: to find their unique route to peace. It was a beautiful and thorough healing.

Near the end of treatment, I explained that they had gained so much wisdom, and that now they had the opportunity to share it. We recorded an audiovisual message for a time capsule to be shared later with their family.

It was rewarding to work with someone so advanced in years and see the relief from so many decades of accumulated trauma.

It's not just about ART. It's about compassion, and inviting passion — *come, passion, come* — into our practice. It's about the way I work and live, and how you work and live.

Veteran

The power of ART can be seen in several sessions I facilitated with a veteran who had been previously identified as treatment resistant, refusing to use evidence-based treatments that had shown progress before. Clinically, we were in a continued stabilization/maintenance treatment phase. They knew I was going to be trained in ART and were open and eager to try this new trauma treatment model.

Through ART, we were able to address their previous trauma. When working with this patient, I kept hearing Laney Rosenzweig's (ART's founder and CEO with RRRC) voice, "Process, not content." This kept me grounded and focussed on my role with ART.

This client did not have specific cogitative memory of their trauma but did have body memory. I remember staying focussed on their body memory for one complete session as their depression was moving to suppressed rage. We moved into the metaphor of the volcano, which erupted for three-quarters of the session.

To their surprise, complete memory of the event evolved through the somatic processing, and they moved out of the frozen state. Staying with the protocol of ART, they were successful in processing this index trauma event, which was ten out of ten SUDS pre-ART, to zero out of ten SUDS (post-test). SUDS is Subjective Units of Distress Scale, a tool for measuring the intensity of internal experiences, such as anxiety, anger, agitation, stress or other psychological pain with ten being the most distressing and zero the least distressing. We dealt with this incident in two sixty-minute ART sessions, and at the end, they began to laugh and said they had let all the pain go. They wondered why they'd held onto this memory for so long. They were able to put the facts into a narrative, as the emotional distress and PTSD symptoms were finally relieved.

Following this, they moved to the transitional phase of treatment and a plan for discharge was made for around two months later.

This was one of the most severe complex trauma cases I'd worked on... and there they were, expressing how they had their life back, and that they were experiencing feelings of joy and hope.

Multiple Traumas

A client had been having psychogenic seizures. Their history was heavily steeped in addiction and trauma around a parent's death. The client had been seen by several other therapists, unsuccessfully.

When I worked with them, the client was waiting for an assessment, but was eager to get going because the seizures were occurring so often that life was unmanageable.

One of the challenges as therapists delivering ART is determining where to go first. In this case, I wanted to stabilize. In addition to the parent's death, there had been a number of other traumatic events.

The client introduced themselves to me with a diagnostic label. "I'm borderline bipolar." That was quite telling for me. We delved into the client's childhood. They'd been attached to the parent who had taken their own life. I asked them, "What happened before shame and guilt showed up?"

I then asked if they had a memory of childhood — a time when they first recalled not feeling safe. The client remembered that around the time they began school, a relative passed away. While at the funeral, their parent (the one who later took their own life) left them with some of the other people there. As the client-child called out for that parent, another family member silenced her with a physical action.

From that day, my client had not been able to ask for what they needed. They had been silenced when calling out what they most needed in that childhood moment of fear and separation.

We worked through ART and the client's seizures stopped. They were able to return to work after being off for a long time. The next year, at a follow up, the client advised me that they were healthy, productive, positive, and an advocate for their own needs. Since that follow up I have received a note that begins with: "Not being my label is fabulous."

Parent Trauma

I worked with a client with a background of complex trauma stemming from childhood trauma, the separation from their own child decades prior, and then the child recently locating them and reaching out. I had utilized evidence-based practice with them, however, they'd been unable to completely resolve their traumas.

Then we engaged in ART. All childhood trauma was resolved, more current issues were surrendered related to the child, and we accomplished this in just three ART sessions. Anxiety and depression lifted. They were finally able to let go and begin to engage in life.

Earthquake Survivor

A client had returned from overseas specifically to participate in ART.

There had been acute trauma experienced during a natural disaster. They had been diagnosed with PTSD and depression.

After two sessions with ART, they reported zero out of ten post-SUDS, as compared to ten out of ten pre-SUDS. They were able to discuss the facts of the disaster but no longer brought up the sensations of anxiety previously suffered. We began working on depression, which had begun in childhood as the client reported a complex history and had also been adopted at birth. As a result of the therapy, the client and their parents reported positive changes in just four ART sessions. Two more sessions occurred, after which they returned—joyfully and with hope—to their home overseas.

ART TESTIMONIALS

> *With one session of ART vs. several of EMDR, I feel that it was much easier to stay present and on point. I also feel that this allowed for results to be achieved more quickly. Keeping my eyes open was very helpful for me to feel that I was maintaining a present state which allowed for me to feel that changes are more real and less of a dream, and/or to achieve a memory more quickly.*

> *ART has been helpful in that it seems to work very fast at relaxing and calming me down. It also seems to help with the events that cause me the most anxiety, usually with just one session.*

> *I feel the ART Program is a success in helping turn my life around into a very positive direction of day-to-day, as well as*

future expectations. My day-to-day changes have been positive and I am alarmingly calm (compared) to what I've experienced. I am less vigilant, less irritable, and less argumentative. I am more calm, relaxed, and carefree about my daily routine, whether scheduled or ad hoc.

As I have experienced positive results from ART, I would like to point out a critical factor that enhances the use of the ART Program for PTSD patients. That critical factor is the aptitude and experience of the trained therapist conducting the program, with the patient. As it is understandable, that all patients' PTSD status is unique, and each character/personality is also unique to each patient.

The Accelerated Resolution Therapy takes the problem away. After we have processed an event or memory, I can move on without that event causing me future distress. Using this method of therapy for memories and, in one case, for a future event, I noticed a great difference in what takes place when I revisit the memory or incident. I can remember the facts, but the outburst of emotion, nervousness, or anxiety either does not manifest itself, or is very minor. I was able to completely change the outcome or ending of the 'troubling scene' or prepare myself for the upcoming future event that I felt was disturbing. ART allows me to retain the facts without becoming emotionally upset and distressed when it is required to think about an incident, or it makes itself present.

I was diagnosed with PTSD. We began the EMDR process one incident at a time. It was an effective process, but I was aware that I was going to be at it for a long time. I had several issues to work through. I also found it to be an extremely emotional process.

Then we started with ART. It was a dramatic change in my processing. I was working through each situation so quickly and the relief and change in my emotions was immediate. I was feeling like the individual situations were almost blocked and irrelevant. What was once a mountain and seemed too big to cover was instantly small and completely manageable. I feel content, sleep better, and function daily with very little thought of the past. I am very happy.

WHAT TO DO BEFORE ART

When you've done what I recommend you do before you deliver ART, then you'll reach the point with your client when ART brings the client to making plans for the future. They will see new horizons because of the freedom they feel. Celebrate that with them.

QUESTIONS

What's your level of ART training? What is your plan to further your ART education?

REFLECTIVE NOTES

SECTION II: YOU, THE THERAPIST

CHAPTER 3

KNOW TRAUMA

It can sometimes feel like the word *trauma* is trending, and from the perspective that it is gaining recognition as a mental health issue that needs attention, that's a good thing. But it doesn't necessarily mean trauma is any more broadly or clearly understood.

Your knowledge of trauma, in all its forms, affects the wellness trajectory of your clients. My aim is to help ensure you are fluent in the language of trauma before you begin ART with your client. As you know, ART works with identified themes and specific incidents/scenes and we'll talk more about that in Chapter 12, *Develop Themes*. Your understanding of trauma types will be critical for your identification of themes and scenes within ART.

Traumatic experiences occur in a variety of environments and situations. They may involve a life-threatening harm such as a near-death accident, a physical harm that wasn't necessarily life threatening, or emotional harm. Trauma has lasting negative effects on the person's physical, mental, and/or emotional health and/or on their social and/or spiritual well-being. Those who are traumatized are at increased risk for further trauma.

There are two categories of trauma. Type 1 trauma is single-incident or acute trauma. Type 1 trauma diagnoses include post-traumatic stress disorder

(PTSD) and complex post-traumatic stress disorder (C-PTSD). The latter was an addition, in 2020, to the World Health Organization's International Classification of Diseases, 11th edition (ICD-11). Type 2 trauma is chronic, prolonged, and repeated. It can occur when a client has been subjected to systematic coercive control by someone, for example:

- Domestic violence
- Child abuse
- Refugee camps
- Cults
- Organized sexual exploitation
- Events surrounding the Holocaust
- Ethnic cleansing
- Systemic rape as a weapon of war
- Arbitrary arrest in totalitarian regimes

Type 2 trauma can also occur from the following:

- Exposure to/victim of violence in armed conflict
- Shortages of basic necessities like food and clean water
- Executions
- Moral injury
- Colonization, where the victim, their family, and community have been disconnected from their culture. (As in Canada's history with the residential school system where children of indigenous families were forcefully taken from the family home and housed in church-run schools.)

The categorization — Type 1 or Type 2 — and the subsequent diagnoses shape the approach a therapist will take.

POST-TRAUMATIC STRESS DISORDER (PTSD)

The Diagnostic and Statistical Manual of Mental Health Disorders Fifth Edition (DSM-5) criteria for PTSD includes, first, direct, or indirect exposure to a traumatic event, followed by symptoms in four categories:

1. Intrusion
2. Avoidance
3. Negative changes in thoughts and mood, and
4. Changes in arousal and reactivity.

It is characterized by an inability to recover after experiencing or witnessing a terrifying event.

PTSD involves the repeated reliving of memories of the traumatic experience in sight, smell, sound, and physical sensation, and is often followed by physiological and psychological stress which may include trembling, crying, fear, rage, confusion, or paralysis, chronic self-destructive behaviours like self-harm, substance abuse, and suicidal behaviours.

Delayed PTSD can occur weeks, months, or years after the event. This can be frightening and confusing as there might not be a clear connection between the symptoms that have developed and become established (a way of life) and the traumatic event.

Severe symptoms occur if the trauma is experienced at an early age, if the trauma was chronic, has impacted brain development or attachment, involved a parent, caregiver, person in position of authority, and/or was profoundly disruptive affecting impacting all the individual's relationships.

COMPLEX POST-TRAUMATIC STRESS DISORDER

Complex PTSD or DESNOS (Disorders of Extreme Stress Not Otherwise Specified) were proposed by Judith Herman, Bessel Van der Kolk, and others, as a revision to the DSM-4 definition of PTSD. This amendment was to identify a syndrome observed in patients who had experienced prolonged and severe repetitive abuse, i.e., Type 2 trauma, most often occurring in childhood. Dr. Herman also identified a group of patients who had experienced cumulative repetitive trauma as adults such as torture or captivity.

The International Classification of Diseases (ICD)-10 also used the term Enduring Personality Change after Catastrophic Experience (EPCACE) to reflect changes in personality brought on by exposure to Type 2 trauma.

The World Health Organization International Classification of Diseases (ICD)-11 describes PTSD and C-PTSD (presented May 2019 / Adoption January 2022) as follows:

> The proposed ICD-11 template comprises, therefore, six disorder-defining criteria: dissociative flashbacks, nightmares, hyper-vigilance, exaggerated startle response, avoidance of external reminders, and avoidance of thoughts and feelings associated with the traumatic event.
>
> — WHO ICD-11

C-PTSD is characterized by three symptom clusters of PTSD, and three clusters reflecting disturbances in self organization (DSO):

- Severe affect dys-regulation (AD)
- Negative self-concept (NSC)
- Persistent disturbance in relationships (DR)

From this information it seems there may now be an accepted, agreed research and clinical diagnostic criteria for Complex PTSD. The official summary is as follows:

> When the ICD-11 was presented at the World Health Assembly in May 2019 for adoption by member states, to come into effect on 1 January 2022, the criteria for C-PTSD

> have a narrow definition and limited number of symptoms. ICD-11 incorporates complex PTSD, not as a separate diagnosis from PTSD but in a hierarchy with PTSD. In ICD-11, complex PTSD, all diagnostic requirements for PTSD are met and, in addition, complex PTSD is characterized by severe and persistent disturbances in self organization (DSO).

C-PTSD can appear as quite a diagnostic mess. It is:

- difficult to diagnose
- increased co-morbidity and functional impairment
- refractory to medications and PTSD psychotherapy treatment
- diagnosis of complex PTSD is predictive of an inhibited treatment response compared to a diagnosis of general PTSD
- high attrition rates to modalities such as EMDR and Prolonged Exposure
- requires prolonged stabilization and trauma treatment which can impact length of treatment.

Clients with C-PTSD will exhibit poor trust. Psychiatric medications that aim to decrease the intensity of symptoms so that therapy can proceed are less effective in patients with complex trauma.

SYMPTOMS OF TRAUMA

There are many causes of trauma and symptoms will manifest differently in each person even if the triggering event is the same. You've recognized the signs of trauma in your practice: avoidance, an exaggerated startle response, irritability, anger, or other negative emotions. Regardless of the type or duration, people with a trauma injury can feel shame, helplessness, powerlessness, intense fear, and anxiety. There will likely be flashbacks to the traumatic events which affects their productivity. Your client may have sleep difficulties: erratic patterns, nightmares, distressing dreams, or insomnia.

They may also blame themselves for some aspect — or all — of the traumatic event.

Trauma is like a virus in the human encoding system; unprocessed traumatic memories can become sticking points that cause mental and physical processes to malfunction. Cellular memory evidence indicates that both the brain and the body's cells can hold an imprint of past traumatic events.

HYPER-AROUSAL AND HYPO-AROUSAL

Hyper-arousal causes traumatized people to react to ordinary frustrations as if they were re-experiencing the traumatic event. The sensations and/or emotions related to the traumatic experiences keep returning and do not fade over time. Clients may not realize that their present intense feelings are related to the past, so they blame the way they feel on their present surroundings or circumstances.

Hyper-arousal creates a feeling of being on edge, reactive, in a state of high alert. It can worsen after experiencing a trauma. This category includes a broad range of physical and psychological symptoms:

- Becoming irritable, quick to anger, or aggressive
- Heightened startle reaction
- Difficulty concentrating
- Frequently scanning the environment or watching for trauma reminders
- Difficulty sleeping
- Feelings of anxiety, and related symptoms such as a racing heart, upset stomach, or headaches
- Risky or impulsive behaviours

Hypo-arousal is the opposite of being reactive. It is the shutting down or collapsing in response to trauma. Hypo-arousal can occur even when there is a perceived threat:

- Numbness and no feelings
- Lack of energy and reduced physical activity
- An inability to process thoughts or answer in a logical way
- Shame, and even
- Dissociation

DISSOCIATION

Trauma can cause the declarative explicit memory processing system to fail in the brain, so the traumatic memory isn't logged and stored properly (just like a computer). The brain (like a supercomputer) reverts to a simpler method of recording signals and encodes traumatic memories as pictures or body sensations.

Memories are split into fragments — like shards of glass — which impede the brain's natural recovery process. Fragments can grow into symptoms associated with PTSD and increase the risk of becoming physically ill.

MORAL INJURY

Moral injury is when someone does or is forced to do something that goes against their beliefs, this is often seen as an act of commission, and when they fail to do something in line with their belief, is called an act of omission. Individuals can experience betrayal from leadership; those in positions of power or peers can cause adverse outcomes. Moral injury is the distressing psychological, behavioural, social and, sometimes, spiritual aftermath of exposure to events that have involved acting, not acting, or witnessing behaviours that go against the individual's values and moral beliefs. The individual then feels like a transgression has occurred, and they or someone else crossed a line with respect to those beliefs. Guilt, disgust, anger, and an inability to self-forgive are strongly evident in moral injury. What follows is engagement in self-sabotaging behaviours — the person may feel they don't deserve to succeed at work or in relationships.

It's important to explore whether a client has incurred one or more moral injuries. Though moral injury is one of the hardest things to deal with, dealing with it is an important piece of healing.

Moral injuries could look something like this (fictional) one: a member of the military is in Bosnia in the role of peacekeeper, which means they are prohibited from fighting in the war. They need to listen to and obey their commanding officer — and the commander says, "Remain neutral." Let's say the member witnesses a child being raped. The rape of a child goes against the member's values, but they have been commanded not to respond. Other scenarios may involve witnessing children maimed by their parents in order for the child to be more successful getting more money from begging. The member wishes to stop that, but they are ordered to stand by and let it happen. The same for treatment of women and children as objects. These assaults against a member's morals create serious internal trauma. Over time, the internal value system of the member — your client — has been assaulted by their duty as a member/soldier/police officer who is following the orders of superiors for the safety of a certain mission.

Eventually, when going against one's values becomes the norm, the quality of service from that person can suffer because the person becomes defeatist; a member of an organization can become more detached, more numb, and apathetic. Over time, hypo-arousal develops; the soldier, officer, paramedic, or front-line nurse feels nothing, so they just go through the routine of the job.

LET'S CLARIFY MORAL AND MORALE BECAUSE THERE MAY BE SOME confusion — whether it is being keystroked or handwritten, and/or transferred by an admin, it's easy to mistakenly throw an E on the end, which changes the whole meaning. If that happens, then our work goes out with an ambiguity associated with the document.

Moral

Moral, as in moral behaviour, refers to core values of what is right or wrong. It involves holding high principles for conduct.

Morale

Morale describes confidence and enthusiasm, as in *to keep up the morale of the group as they reach the summit.*

Morale, of course, is often affected when morals are challenged, attacked, ignored when working in an institutional structure — hence many populations suffer moral injuries, and the morale of the unit or group is eroded because of that.

Both words, moral and morale, are related to ethics and values but they don't mean the same thing.

COGNITIVE DISTORTION

Clients with deeply buried trauma will have had irrational thoughts influence their emotions — the whiteboard work of before, now, and after illustrates the variation in their perceptions and understandings directly related to their life. Some of your clients will have more extreme thoughts which will raise a red flag for you. Always assess for cognitive distortions. They include:

Magnification and minimization: Exaggerating or minimizing the importance of events. One might believe their own achievements are unimportant, or that their mistakes are excessively important.

Catastrophizing: Seeing only the worst possible outcomes of a situation.

Overgeneralization: Making broad interpretations from a single or few events. "I felt awkward during my job interview. I am always so awkward."

Magical thinking: The belief that acts will influence unrelated situations. "I am a good person – bad things shouldn't happen to me."

PERSONALIZATION: The belief that one is responsible for events outside of their own control. "My mom is always upset. She would be fine if I did more to help her."

JUMPING TO CONCLUSIONS: Interpreting the meaning of a situation with little or no evidence.

MIND READING: Interpreting the thoughts and beliefs of others without adequate evidence. "She would not go on a date with me. She probably thinks I'm ugly."

FORTUNE TELLING: The expectation that a situation will turn out badly without adequate evidence.

EMOTIONAL REASONING: The assumption that emotions reflect the way things really are. "I feel like a bad friend, therefore I must be a bad friend."

DISQUALIFYING THE POSITIVE: Recognizing only the negative aspects of a situation while ignoring the positive. One might receive many compliments on an evaluation, but focus on the single piece of negative feedback.

"SHOULD" STATEMENTS: The belief that things should be a certain way. "I should always be friendly."

ALL-OR-NOTHING THINKING: Thinking in absolutes such as "always," "never," or "every." "I never do a good enough job on anything."

Examine cognitive distortions and familiarize yourself with cognitive framework:

- Explore your client's cognitions — values and beliefs — *before* joining the organization.
- Explore your client's values and beliefs *now* regarding changes — safety, world, self-esteem.
- Ask how the client would like to see their cognitions — values and beliefs — in the *future.*
- Ask your clients when they noticed a shift and change.

TRAUMA-INFORMED CARE

Trauma-informed care, or trauma-informed therapy, refers to the way a therapist will customize an individual's needs based on their trauma history, triggers, and needs, versus the actual service of providing intervention. In a perfect world, all care organizations would engage in trauma-informed care.

Trauma therapy clients can feel that everything is falling apart — and often it is — because of their inability to regulate emotions and navigate relationships. Your understanding of their needs is a separate entity from your knowledge of trauma itself.

The key in trauma-informed care is to view one client at a time, and not to generalize — a separate lens for each client. In our industry, there is training to understand how to approach treatment through a trauma-informed lens.

Trauma-informed therapy takes into consideration a client's experiences as to how trauma has an effect on behaviour, mental health, and the client's ability to participate in treatment. Therapists undertake to work from a trauma-informed lens by engaging without triggering or re-traumatizing.

What does that mean for you?

It means that you understand all aspects of trauma and can separate symptoms from trauma without getting caught up in treating the symptoms. It means you recognize the widespread impact of trauma and comprehend the potential paths for healing without re-triggering the trauma. You'll notice the signs and symptoms of trauma in clients, and in staff, interns, residents, and others in the system; even within yourself. When you do see it, you will respond by fully integrating your knowledge about trauma into the policies, procedures, practices, and settings of the organization you are representing. When you operate from a trauma-informed lens, you affiliate with other trauma-informed service providers, systems, and organizations.

The core trauma-informed principles are:

- Acknowledge the practice
- Recognition that trauma is pervasive

- Safety
- Trust
- Choice
- Control
- Compassion

The problem is that many clinicians are not trained to adopt a trauma-informed lens of practice. The Canadian system does not operate from a trauma-informed lens. Yet. I can always be hopeful.

TREATING TRAUMA

I explain in training that we only see the tip of the iceberg: what is visible above the ocean is only a fraction of what lies below. Icebergs symbolize a large group of clients: people who are emotionally numb or suspend their belief of symptoms. Many will deny symptoms when first interviewed. The denial can be so convincing that you might wonder why the person has been referred for assessment of trauma. Ninety per cent of what is happening to the client, and their symptoms, lies beneath the surface. They will have often experienced severe and repetitive trauma, but they may present as not fully meeting the DSM diagnostic criteria for PTSD at the first interview. It is vital not to miss this, not to negate a diagnosis and dismiss the patient, or mislabel the patient as having a personality disorder, when they are presenting with the symptoms of trauma and, indirectly but as best they can, asking for help.

Meet your client where they are. You may be well versed on the treatments available for trauma — you may even have the training to deliver those modalities — but it is unlikely your clients are. Neither will they be aware, nor do they have to be aware, of the diagnostic criteria against which their symptoms have been or must be evaluated.

The most common treatments for trauma include:

- Cognitive behavioural therapy: CBT is a common and well-supported treatment for trauma disorders. CBT works by

identifying and challenging unhealthy thinking patterns that contribute to the symptoms of trauma. The proven benefits of CBT can be long-lasting.
- Exposure therapy: During exposure therapy, the patient is exposed to reminders of their trauma in a gradual and safe way. With enough exposure, the trauma begins to lose its emotional power, and the symptoms dismiss. Exposure therapies have extensive research support and include: eye movement desensitization and reprocessing (EMDR) and Prolonged Exposure. Other treatments, such as narrative exposure therapy, and group therapy have all been found to be helpful for survivors of trauma.
- Medication: Medication may be used to manage the symptoms of trauma, such as anxiety, depression, and insomnia. It can be especially valuable when a person's symptoms are so intense that they are unable to participate in psychotherapy. Note, the medication is for the symptoms; the source of the trauma remains an entity unto itself. The trauma is what ART addresses.

Inform your client of what type of therapies you're trained in. Make sure to define terms, share your understanding of how it feels to be traumatized, and ask your client how it feels for them. I encourage you and each of your clients to read the work of trauma pioneer, Dr. Robert Scaer, *Healing Trauma and the Power of the Human Spirit.* Consider supporting your client to put their own version into words or a sketch. It can be a way to individualize your approach to your client. It can help them find a voice through a pen.

WATCH FOR THE LOOP

It's easy to get off track when you are working with clients who present symptoms in the session. What do I mean? You may find yourself in a loop, going over the same things with your client. (Sometimes this might be a scene match — we will talk about this in Chapter 12.) The following checklist can help you avoid the trap of treating the symptoms the client is presenting, to stay on track of dealing with the trauma, and to remind you of the symptoms to address after the trauma work is done.

Physical symptoms include:

- Fatigue
- Irritability
- GI distress
- Headaches
- Tension
- Dis-ease
- Weakened immune system
- Pain

Emotional and cognitive symptoms include:

- Anxiety, depression
- Difficulty concentrating
- Anger
- Sadness
- Pessimism/cynicism
- Judgement of self/others
- Forgetfulness
- Self-destructiveness

Behavioural symptoms include:

- Aggression
- Avoidance
- Overeating
- Alcohol/drug use
- Isolation
- Perfectionism
- Sarcasm
- Excessive risk-taking
- Volatility

Spiritual and relational symptoms include:

- Hopelessness
- Disconnection
- Self-loathing
- Guilt and shame
- Lack of joy
- Fearfulness

Some of us have been trained in the science of trauma and the brain, while others are skilled in emotional counselling and have less brain biology in their educational history. But each of us needs to understand all aspects of trauma so that we are able to build our therapy plans and explain it to clients.

QUESTIONS

Why is it important to stay "out of the loop" to focus on treating the trauma?

REFLECTIVE NOTES

CHAPTER 4

THE BIOLOGY OF THE BRAIN

The brain is like a supercomputer whose job is, at least partly, to process, encode, organize, and store information about memories and experiences. The information we take in is captured through an electronic action that connects nerves between the brain and the body. The body then speaks to the brain through this electronic setup and gives its feedback to the input the brain sent. This electronic handshake takes place via a space that is like a bridge between two nerve cells; a tiny space across which impulses are transferred via what scientists call a neurotransmitter. The neurotransmitter being a chemical substance that facilitates the arrival of a message across the gap between nerve fibres, muscle fibres, or other structures that are receptors.

This entire system is recorded and as feelings and responses, hence: the body remembers. They are referenced later when we are reminded of specific situations. Some of those situations are described as pleasant. Others are extremely unpleasant.

The physical organ that is the brain weighs about three pounds, its folding surface accounting for half the brain's weight. It contains blood vessels, nerves, glial cells, and a complex network of about 100 billion neurons. It's about 60 per cent fat and 40 per cent water, protein, carbohydrates, and salts. And it controls every process that regulates our body.

THOSE LITTLE GREY CELLS

Two types of matter are found in the brain: grey matter and white matter. The grey matter is composed of round, central cell bodies called neuron somas and is found on the outside of the brain. The grey matter forms the cerebral cortex, which is primarily responsible for the cognitive abilities, processing and interpreting information, setting us apart from all other living creatures.

The white matter is the inner section under the grey matter. It is made of long stems that connect neurons together, called axons, wrapped in an insulating, protective sheath called myelin. In the spinal cord, the white is on the outside and the grey sits within, while white matter transmits that information to other parts of the nervous system.

THE AMYGDALA

Amygdala is Latin for almond — owing to the fact it is shaped like an almond. The amygdala is located within the temporal lobe and contains a group of neurons believed to work together to perform certain functions as part of the limbic system — a system which includes the hippocampus (related to memory), and cingulate gyrus (related to emotion). It's referred to in singular form, but there are two amygdalae, one in each cerebral hemisphere. The temporal lobe itself is associated with memory, language, and hearing.

The amygdala is always on duty. It is the frontline of our biological response team and functions in all situations, constantly scanning for threats. Any threat — real, perceived, or remembered — is immediately processed by the amygdala. It releases norepinephrine, a hormone and chemical messenger (neurotransmitter), sending messages to the cerebral cortex and on to the rest of the brain to trigger a fight, flight, or freeze response. Truly dangerous situations require less than split-second action — escaping a fire, diving out of the way of a bullet, running from a grizzly — and so that frontline response kicks in without the benefit of the perceived threat being evaluated.

In situations where a person has been traumatized, the amygdala relives the threat and sends messages, over and over, that there is danger when there is not.

This is how I explain it to clients: when someone cuts me off in traffic, my amygdala says, "Hey! That guy cut me off!" My stress rises quickly. Then it comes down quickly. My stress was around zero, quickly shot up to near ten, then returned to zero just as fast and I started thinking about the dinner I was going to enjoy. But, for someone with PTSD, the baseline is not zero and has not been at zero for a while. It has never fully come down from the stressful and traumatic situation it went through. There's not much wiggle room and so being cut off in traffic triggers a response likely out of proportion to the event. That's the amygdala at work.

HIPPOCAMPUS

The word hippocampus comes from the Greek word for seahorse, which is what its shape resembles. The brain has two hippocampi, one in each hemisphere. The hippocampus is vital to the formation of memory. It's the part of the brain most affected by Alzheimer's Disease. Researchers have also noted that reduced volume of the hippocampus is seen in patients with depression and with PTSD. Hippocampal injury can result from head injury, stroke, seizures, brain tumours, drug withdrawal, Alzheimer's, and from exposure to intense, continuous stress. Studies in the National Library of Science have shown that hippocampal injuries typically evolve into cognitive dysfunction, depression, and/or epilepsy.

PREFRONTAL CORTEX

The prefrontal cortex, as the name suggests, sits right at the front of the brain. It is divided into the dorsolateral prefrontal cortex and the orbitofrontal cortex. Responsible for higher-level thinking, reasoning, planning, and self-development, the prefrontal cortex is integral to making decisions, troubleshooting, managing emotions, and applying intelligence. This area governs our consciousness, and is associated with cognitive disorders linked to hyperactivity, autism, bipolar, depression, and schizophrenia. Individuals with PTSD have been found to have decreased function of the prefrontal cortex when exposed to traumatic triggers. They become overly aroused and are on high alert, which can make it hard to relax and to sleep. Once again, we discover a part of the physical body which is directly affected by PTSD.

VAGUS NERVE AND POLYVAGAL THEORY

The vagus nerve, or tenth cranial nerve, is the longest nerve with many branches wandering throughout the body. Some call it the third brain.

It interfaces with the parasympathetic nervous system and is associated with control of the heart, lungs, and digestive tract.

The polyvagal theory, proposed by Stephen Porges in 1994, suggests this system is directly related to emotion regulation, social connection, and fear and response.

BRAIN HEMISPHERES

The brain is comprised of two halves joining at an inter-hemispheric fissure. The right hemisphere controls the left side of the body, and the left half controls the right side of the body. The two halves are in contact with each other via a large, C-shaped structure of white matter and nerve pathways called the corpus callosum. The corpus callosum is in the centre of the cerebrum.

The brainstem (middle of brain) connects the cerebrum with the spinal cord. The brainstem includes the midbrain, the pons and the medulla. The midbrain (mesencephalon) is a complex structure with neuron clusters and neural pathways.

The pons — Latin for bridge — is the origin for four of the twelve cranial nerves, which enable a range of activities such as tear production, chewing, blinking, focusing vision, balance, hearing and facial expression. The pons is the connection between the midbrain and the medulla.

The medulla is at the bottom of the brainstem, where the brain meets the spinal cord. The medulla is essential to survival. Functions of the medulla regulate many bodily activities, including heart rhythm, breathing, blood flow, and oxygen and carbon dioxide levels. The medulla produces reflexive activities such as sneezing, vomiting, coughing, and swallowing.

The cerebellum — little brain — is the size of a fist and located at the back of the head below the temporal and occipital lobes. It has two hemispheres. The outer portion contains neurons, and the inner area communicates with the cerebral cortex. It coordinates voluntary muscle movements to maintain posture and balance.

Each brain hemisphere (parts of the cerebrum) has four sections, called lobes: frontal, parietal, temporal, and occipital. Each lobe controls specific functions.

- The frontal lobe is the largest — personality characteristics, decision-making, movement, smell recognition, and speech ability within the Broca area (which is within the frontal lobe).
- The parietal lobe is the middle part of the brain — it helps with object identification, spatial relationships, and interpreting pain and touch. Inside the parietal lobe is the Wernicke's area which helps the brain understand spoken language.
- The occipital lobe is the back part of the brain and it's involved with vision.
- The temporal lobes are at the sides of the brain. They are involved in short term memory, rhythm, and some smell recognition.

Deeper structures in the brain are the pituitary gland (master gland), the hypothalamus (body temperature, hunger), pineal gland (sleep).

Two sets of blood vessels supply blood and oxygen to the brain: the vertebral arteries and the carotid arteries. The external carotid arteries run up the side of the neck — note: that's where you feel your pulse. The vertebral arteries follow the spinal column into the skull, where they join at the brainstem and form the basilar artery, which supplies blood to the rear portions of the brain. The circle of Willis is a loop of blood vessels near the bottom of the brain that connects the major arteries.

CRANIAL NERVES

Inside the cranium, the dome of the skull, are twelve cranial nerves:

- Cranial nerve 1: olfactory nerve — sense of smell
- Cranial nerve 2: optic nerve — eyesight
- Cranial nerve 3: oculomotor nerve — pupil response and other motions of the eye
- Cranial nerve 4: trochlear — muscles in the eye
- Cranial nerve 5: trigeminal nerve (largest and most complex) – sensory and motor function
- Cranial nerve 6: abducens nerve — eye muscles
- Cranial nerve 7: facial nerve — movement, taste, glandular functions
- Cranial nerve 8: vestibulocochlear — balance and hearing
- Cranial nerve 9: glossopharyngeal nerve — taste, ear and throat movement, and other functions
- Cranial nerve 10: vagus nerve — ear and the digestive system and controls motor activity in the heart, throat, and digestive system
- Cranial nerve 11: accessory nerve — specific muscles in the head, neck, and shoulder
- Cranial nerve 12: hypoglossal nerve — motor activity to the tongue

The first two nerves originate in the cerebrum. The other ten emerge from the brainstem.

Knowledge of the brain is necessary for trauma work, even when you are seemingly only dealing with emotional issues.

QUESTIONS

How comfortable are you with the biology of the brain? What areas will you note to do further reading on?

Why is knowledge of the brain necessary for trauma therapy work?

REFLECTIVE NOTES

CHAPTER 5

ATTACHMENT, DEVELOPMENT, AVOIDANCE

Attachment is the emotional bond connecting us to others. It is not always equal, affected by nature, nurture, and environmental circumstances. How your clients present their challenges to you and your approach to their treatment will be influenced by their level of attachment, their stage of development (not age), and their patterns of avoidance.

THEORIES OF ATTACHMENT

John Bowlby proposed a theory of attachment in the 1950s and 1960s. He suggested that the quality of the bond between a baby and its caregiver or parent affects that child's emotional life in later years.

He identified four attachment types: secure, anxious-ambivalent, avoidant, and disorganized.

- Secure attachment represents a warm and loving bond and the ability to form healthy relationships with others. An individual with secure attachment is confident in their interactions with others. This security is carried into adulthood; individuals who

developed secure attachment do not appear to have problems in long-term relationships (no fear of abandonment).
- Anxious-ambivalent attachment reflects lack of trust, in particular of parents or caregivers. This may show up as fear over a situation when that same situation would excite a secure person. Those exhibiting anxious-ambivalent constantly seek approval from their parents/caregivers. They are vigilant about observation — they watch their surroundings because they fear they will be abandoned. (Later, they can feel unloved by their partners.) They can be quite dependent as adults.
- Avoidant attachment represents those who have learned that their emotional needs are likely going to be unmet. They often struggle with expressing feelings and find it hard to understand emotions. As adults they may avoid intimate relationships.
- Disorganized attachment combines avoidant and anxious attachment. This group will often display anger or rage. Those who angrily broke toys and possessions in their early years may well be the ones as adults who easily explode and have a tough time controlling their emotions.

Next came Bowen, whose Family of Origin theory both challenged and overlapped Bowlby.

Bowen focussed on attachment in childhood, and he conceptualized a family of origin as a living, emotional ecosystem which creates each person's self-image, values, behaviours, attitudes, and the way they relate to others. The family system defines the flow of emotional process or patterns of emotional functioning in a nuclear family.

Bowen's model views people within the context of a larger multigenerational system or network that defines roles people have, expectations they develop, and rules a person follows. Ultimately the family is the main source of knowledge, attitudes, and roles through example and words — the stories we are told. These attachment patterns become the habits of adulthood.

Bowen's family theory supports a differentiation-of-self approach that defines the way a person connects to family and how they establish their independence or autonomy. He developed a scale of differentiation that measures an individual's balance between togetherness and independence on a scale of 0 - 100.

People at the low end of the range (1 - 25), live in a feeling world, unable to differentiate between thoughts and feelings. Decisions are based on what feels right and responses can range from automatic compliance to extreme oppositional behaviour.

At the top of the range, 95 - 100, are the principle-oriented and goal directed, secure within themselves, able to listen without reacting, respect the identity of others and enjoy relationships. Bowen's model allows people to see others more objectively, as well as themselves, and brings an awareness of attachment patterns that help therapists demonstrate the issues a client is dealing with.

THEORY OF DEVELOPMENT

Psychologist Erik Erikson developed one of the most influential theories of development. His theory centred on psychosocial development. Erikson's stages are:

1. Trust versus mistrust. From birth to about eighteen months an infant develops trust through the reliability and consistency of care. When this isn't happening, then the ability to develop trust will be impacted, thus leading to mistrust.
2. Autonomy versus shame and doubt. From eighteen months to approximately age two or three years old, the child develops a sense of independence and some personal control over physical skills. Based on this, if parents do not allow their children to explore — and with positive feedback for failure — then there will develop shame and doubt. Remember, success at that age leads to feelings of autonomy.

3. Initiative versus guilt. Between three and five years old, the child asserts control and power by planning activities, and coming up against challenges. This helps them develop a sense of purpose. If they are controlled or harshly criticized (shamed) they can develop guilt.
4. Industry versus inferiority. At five to about twelve years old, the child's peers will become more significant and a major source of self-esteem. New social demands will need to be coped with. This is a make-or-break stage for a sense of competence or inferiority.
5. Identity versus confusion. In the teenage years, from twelve to eighteen, there is an exploration of "who am I?" The teen seeks to establish the sense of self. They will experiment with roles, activities, and behaviours. Erikson theorizes this process is key to forming a strong identity and developing a sense of direction in life.
6. Intimacy versus isolation. In young adulthood, from age nineteen to about forty, there are challenging areas to be traversed — forming loving relationships being a major one. Strong relationships will allow for resilience and success; loneliness, even isolation, will result from failure.
7. Generativity versus stagnation. Between forty and sixty-five years old, there is a need to create legacy. Often that will be a positive change that will benefit other people. When successful, there will be feelings of usefulness, of achievement. The opposite will result in a shallow connection with the world.
8. Integrity versus despair. After sixty-five years old comes the time to measure the satisfaction. If successful during this stage, the person will feel wise. The reverse will result in a deep sense of regret or even bitterness and despair.

SUMMARY OF DEVELOPMENT

The purpose of Erikson's stages is to provide a framework within which development can be considered. Erikson himself emphasized his work was a tool used in our thinking rather than a factual analysis. The strength of the theory is that it allows us to tie together psychosocial development across the entire lifespan. Erikson's developmental stages can help you understand where your client might be. Your knowledge of patterns of attachment will be of great help too. Within that client's complex trauma, you will be able to comprehend your client's distress of their current situation, then go into the childhood.

AVOIDANCE

There is putting things off until another (better) time... and there is avoidance. The first is a normal part of the human experience. The second is a maladaptive avoidance and a mental health concern. When thoughts and emotions become unbearable, avoidance activities become or generate a whole new problem.

Any action that is carried out to prevent discomfort like sadness, shame, or fear is avoidant behaviour.

Avoidance may be an effective strategy in the short term, but not in the long term; not, for example, when it looks like substance abuse.

Avoidance is a distinctive part of adaptive and maladaptive fear. Adaptive fear is exampled when a person would not approach a grizzly bear, or not go into the ocean after a shark attack. This is a healthy response. But avoidance in the absence of a real threat can damage a person's quality of life and prevent them from correcting their anxiety. This is maladaptive avoidance, recognized by the World Health Organization and the American Psychiatric Association, for example, as a characteristic of a spectrum of mental disorders.

The symptoms of avoidance include:

- avoiding people and even loved ones who are reminders of the trauma
- feeling disconnected or distant from reality
- refusing to participate in activities that relate to the trauma (i.e., driving a car, visiting a hospital, etc.)
- not feeling pain or physical sensations within one's body
- avoiding memories from the trauma
- shutting down emotionally and having a difficult time expressing love
- distancing oneself from activities that used to be enjoyable.

When PTSD is involved, avoidance can begin to look like regression and isolation to cope with painful reminders. Avoidance behaviours are associated with increased severity of PTSD symptoms.

Emotional avoidance is part of the avoidance cluster of PTSD symptoms. Patients and clients will want to avoid distressing memories as well as external visual reminders or conversations about the event. Emotional numbing symptoms such as feeling distant from others, losing interest in activities the client formerly enjoyed, are common coping mechanisms. Research shows that people with PTSD push away their emotions which results in development of even more PTSD symptoms.

When a person avoids thoughts or feelings about a traumatic event, that kind of avoidance is internal. It looks like this: someone who has experienced a sexual assault may avoid even healthy relationships. A combat veteran may shut down feelings of sadness about a specific war zone in which they were deployed. That kind of internal avoidance is a massive emotional upheaval.

An earthquake survivor may turn to alcohol to avoid memories of the time when their home was destroyed. They may find that using substances helps numb the feelings they experienced when they lost their home. But, after a time, the problems that occur in the person's life are those related to the substances. All treatment will then be directed toward the coping mechanism: substance abuse used to avoid the memories of the loss of their home.

A person experiencing PTSD might find that they are pushing back or fighting against therapy so that the PTSD can remain in a priority position; they may find they use all their energy to avoid certain emotions which then makes it difficult to manage other experiences. All their energy goes into managing avoidance and carrying the burden of chronic worry.

YOU ARE NOT YOUR...

There are all kinds of circumstances that can lead to avoidance. For example, a diagnosis for a serious illness is distressing, tragic, and even traumatic. The disease can become a label by which the patient (already a label) is identified. You can watch for this in your clients and listen to their language — I am a diabetic, I am an alcoholic, I am morbidly obese, I am damaged, I am broken. And you can correct them: You are a person who has diabetes. You are a person who is heavier than average.

QUESTIONS

How do you understand attachment in your own history?

Could this result in bias when you're dealing with clients?

How do you ensure you are clear about avoidance in your own life?

How do you recognize avoidant behaviours in your clients' lives (in order to separate symptoms from the root trauma)?

REFLECTIVE NOTES

CHAPTER 6

CULTURAL COMPETENCE & SPECIALIZED POPULATIONS

Just as trauma is categorized into types for diagnosis, your client will be a member of one or more specialized populations with a culture unique to that population. In this chapter we're going to talk about both cultural competence and specialized populations.

CULTURAL COMPETENCE

Specialized populations in ART refer to people who belong to a broad group which is vulnerable to trauma incidents due to the nature of the group. This includes first responders, refugees, and children.

Cultural competence is the ability of a person to effectively interact, work, and develop meaningful relationships with people of differing cultural backgrounds and the inherent beliefs, customs, and behaviours of their culture.

Developing cultural competence is a process that includes developing skills to recognize and respect the diversity around us through the words we speak and the actions we take. There are five components to cultural competency:

1. Having an open attitude
2. Being self-aware
3. Being aware of others
4. Having cultural knowledge, and
5. Possessing cultural skills

Ultimately, cultural competence is the awareness that a peaceful globalization requires of us to understand each other.

The world's population has always been diverse. People have adapted to their geographical regions and followed the ways of their leaders. For millennia, the lifestyles, values, and beliefs of one population didn't overlap with another. Today, that is no longer the case. Our world is a mosaic, and cultural diversity a positive which enriches our globalization. Problems occur when people do not take into consideration cultural norms that will affect our interactions with each other.

When cultural competence is not encouraged or practiced by therapists, discrimination and bias add to the issues that traumatized clients already carry. This has serious consequences since some of the people we treat are holding on by a thread.

Gaining cultural competence is a process. No one reaches a point where they decide they understand it all. Here is a list of things you can do to increase your cultural competence with clients:

- Actively listen. The best thing we can do is to listen to those whose culture is different than ours.
- Critique your own bias — examine your background.
- Ask open ended questions without bias. Be curious.
- Ask and learn about the native language spoken by your client and their community.
- Learn about the child-rearing, religious traditions, and roles of extended family.
- Gather information on days of celebration and acknowledge them.

Cultural competence may lead to tolerance but it is not the same thing. Tolerance infers that someone is putting up with something. Cultural competence is open-mindedly and without judgement learning about others. This requires empathy — that quality of seeing and feeling an event that another is going through. To empathize doesn't mean to agree, it means acknowledge the validity of feelings. When you've done that, engagement comes next. Engagement is an extension of active listening and empathy, and together they help ensure each interaction is smooth and respectful.

When I was working with soldiers who had served one or more tours of duty in Bosnia, I researched the Bosnia war crime trials so that I could get a greater understanding of what my clients had been exposed to. I have also used Google Earth to review physical locations that are significant for clients, and other types of exploration that help me conceptualize the experience my client is grappling with.

To be invested in the roles and populations of clients is to sit with them and hold them in their suffering.

SPECIALIZED POPULATIONS

Your therapy decisions will be based on the dynamics of the specialized population to which the client belongs, the trauma common to that group and the trauma specific to the individual you are working with. There are overlaps in specialized populations; you may treat a first responder who was abused as a child and therefore take that into consideration when you work on the assessment. You'll begin to understand where your client is emotionally stuck, and you'll get to know which situation is causing the most distress. It is possible to dive deep into dissecting highly targeted specialized populations. However, I'm going to address and describe a few key ones.

- Front line/first responders/medical professionals
- Refugees and immigrants
- Seniors
- Indigenous populations, e.g., survivors of the residential school system
- Chronically ill and terminally ill
- Children
- Youth in foster care or those who have aged out
- Youth with a parent who is a member of the armed forces on active duty
- Therapists

FRONT-LINE FIRST RESPONDERS

Soldiers, police, emergency medical service providers (both onsite and at hospitals), firefighters, search and rescue team members, grief counsellors at mass-casualty events, medical examiners, staff at victim services, journalists, and crime scene personnel are among an long list of first responders who can and do receive trauma diagnoses. Many more subcategories exist within these groups, including the volunteer and paid workers who help first responder professions.

The professions, within first responders or related to first responders, also include personnel from other units, like traffic, crime scene investigators, and others who collect and analyze crime scene evidence and information. They may experience trauma as part of their roles in special projects such as strikes, major national or international sporting events, security and protection.

Their assignments could include:

- Hostage negotiations
- Undercover work
- Domestics
- Major crimes
- Special operations
- Impaired driving
- Terrorism
- Torture
- Natural disasters
- Court workers
- Bomb disarming and disposal

Members of these specialized populations may suffer trauma because of exposure to:

- Sudden death: natural, suicide, collisions, violence (shootings, falls/accidents, first-responder deaths, sudden infant death syndrome, murder)
- Physical, emotional, psychological, or sexual abuse; neglect, ritual abuse, torture, abduction
- Organizational moral injury (mistrust, betrayal, anger, shame, guilt): sexual, bullying, harassment, environmental, racism, gender discrimination
- Loss and grief: traumatic, disenfranchised, complicated grief
- Medical: emotional and physical disabilities, and physical pain

When working with these individuals, you'll need to take the following into account:

- Addictions: alcohol; prescribed or illegal drugs; gambling; pornography; shopping
- Homicidal and suicidal ideation: attempts — how, when, outcome
- Previous childhood trauma: sexual abuse, physical abuse
- Dismissal from a position or organization

REFUGEE/IMMIGRANT POPULATION

Traumatized refugees are fighting for the most basic level of survival, and you will want to understand their innate drive to live. Their way of living may appear similar, on the outside, to others — they will mimic the actions of nesting in a home and obtaining things for that home (regardless of where home is). They will explore their surroundings, but they are within a special population for whom certain actions are necessary for survival while dealing with severe fallout from trauma.

Refugees have basic needs and additionally require reminders that they are seen, and they are wanted. They need this from those in their new country — a country which said, "Come, it's safe for you here."

On December 3, 2018, Canada's *The Globe and Mail* reported on Yazidi refugees and the trauma they carry. The article, written by Christina Frangou and photographed by Kiana Hayeri, documented the trauma of Jihan, a young woman who continued to experience trauma-related seizures years after her escape from Islamic State captors.

Given that two-thirds of female Yazidi refugees who survived savagery by ISIS experience a somatic symptom disorder — physical symptoms (in this case seizures) which cannot be explained by an existing medical condition — Jihan is part of a specialized population that continues to grow and whose members become clients of Western trauma practitioners.

We are part of a global population in which many are exposed to levels of inhumanity perpetrated by powerful regimes. We live in a violent world in which there is a constant stream of asylum-seeking people, therefore a continual resettling. In these days of escalating war, shifting borders, newly landed residents are in need and deserve care to deal with their trauma.

SENIORS

Senior citizens can feel that society is biased against them, that they are disposable, unimportant, or too old for treatment. They've gone from being revered in younger years when they were mentors and active contributors to society, but when they need healing relief from trauma suffered in their childhood, youth, or adulthood, society's treatment can leave them feeling like their value is being ignored. Or discounted.

Do not stereotype a senior client. If they can cognitively hang onto a thought, and they are somewhat aware there are triggers, they deserve a life review and should be afforded the opportunity to deal with earlier trauma. Being able to reset as a senior allows for the same level of fresh-transition to tomorrow as it does with others. Additionally, it helps with meaning-making for the future.

One of the things I noticed while I was director at a hospice organization was that individuals who had trauma in their past — and had not been diagnosed with PTSD, therefore not received therapy — was that they would have horrendous nightmares. Here they were in palliative care, preparing for their transition from life, and they had unfinished business. I witnessed them delay their transition (delay dying).

What we carry with us can impact our end-of-life experience. That is why there should be no age limit on receiving therapy to deal with trauma. My experiences in end-of-life care made an outspoken advocate out of me so that people could deal with their trauma, rather than take it to the end of their life. I advised veterans and others, "Do the work now so it doesn't haunt you at the end of life." That is a vital awareness piece because we are all going to age and if we don't work with the trauma, it will impact our functioning.

INDIGENOUS POPULATIONS

Currently in Canada, and other countries which have displaced their indigenous populations, there are many people who are suffering the effects of generational trauma.

Inuit, Metis, and First Nations people are the recognized indigenous groups in Canada. Marginalized since settlers arrived, they face numerous issues in their communities on treaty land, or in centres which exist on colonized land. As stereotypes abound, and opportunities are denied indigenous peoples, communities become isolated, and coping mechanisms (for trauma) like substance abuse increase. Canadians have been on a mission to acknowledge those who were displaced; they face the task of reconciliation for the events of the past, and to work to create a resolution in which all violent and hateful actions are acknowledged, and stereotypes are eliminated.

Included in these events is the horror of residential schools and the practices therein. The last one ceased to operate in 1996. The first federal one began operating in 1883, though before confederation, 1867, regional residential schools go back to the 1830s. Government sanctioned, and wholly operated with Catholic and Anglican backing, the system was barbaric.

In 1987, a series of events took place which brought to light the horrific practices that had taken place in the past — and not too far past — regarding residential schools. This led to identifying perpetrators in the system who had physically and sexually abused indigenous children — in one case, 140-700 incidents were linked solely to one supervisor at one school. Criminal proceedings started, as did the coming to terms of what settlers had caused an entire population, and the understanding that an entire population of indigenous were continuing to suffer and experience trauma due to actions, sanctioned by the government, that had taken place in the past.

Your work as a therapist in ART will likely include, at some time, planning and sessions with a client who has been a victim of these or other crimes of the past, and the continued generational trauma.

When you do work with this population, hone your cultural competence, become aware of the issues through study, and check any propensity to marginalize or stereotype as you become a key component of a healing journey. Your clients may overlap into other categories, and exhibit symptoms that may seem insurmountable to deal with, but your cultural competence combined with familiarity of the therapy, will allow you to help heal open wounds.

CHRONICALLY ILL AND TERMINALLY ILL

When we think of end of life, palliative care, or hospice, we often think about people who have lived decades and experienced every phase of life. Our view might be different for chronic illness. What we tend to forget is that those who have chronic illnesses, have been given a terminal diagnosis, can be any age. The illnesses and the interventions received for those illnesses may be traumatic. People in this category, no matter their age or career, are a specialized population.

The concept of hospice and palliative care leads us away from the topics of pain and fear, there is still a lot to unpack around unfinished business and trauma incurred prior to the diagnosis, that led to the illness or condition, and the shock of the diagnosis. Yet trauma therapy is not often introduced as an option to the time remaining in survivorship.

Underrepresented for articles and studies, trauma care for those who are chronically ill or terminally ill, this specialized population are new-ish to the list.

Your involvement in providing ART to those who are in this population will likely be delivered alongside ongoing medical care. Recognize that trauma is not always acknowledged when end of life events are taking place, be it a hospice stay, palliative care given in the home, or ongoing chronically ill client. Know that while your clients can be any age, older individuals may carry a larger burden of trauma exposure. No matter the age, the trauma suffered from chronic illness medical trauma, or a terminal illness can negatively affect mental health. Pain becomes a burden on the client as well; this can affect the participation in therapy.

Make sure that you are thorough in your assessment — trauma history

— when you are providing compassionate adjunct therapy to an already busy patient who is dealing with multiple care routines.

MEDICAL ASSISTANCE IN DYING (MAID)

In Canada, there is a program through which a qualified professional assists an individual, at the individual's request, to intentionally end their life with the aid of drugs. The Medical Assistance in Dying program (MAiD) involves at least three months of work and administration assessing each application for this medically-assisted death. In therapy, we deal with those who have suicide ideation, but it was a new one for me, recently, when I was asked to work with someone who had been officially approved to die with assistance.

The client had gone to great lengths to obtain permission. They had done their work and were determined to follow through, adamant that nothing would reverse their decision because of the extreme physical and emotional pain that accompanied a medical condition. While the client had obtained the support of medical professionals in their pursuit of MAiD, one of the doctors asked the client if they'd consider ART. The client agreed, since they'd already been accepted under MAiD.

It was interesting for me that the client's history — pre-medical diagnosis and the cause of the MAiD application — had been filled with trauma — unresolved, even unrecognized, trauma.

The client responded to ART. As the amygdala reset, the earlier traumas processed and the client achieved a new clarity and began to re-evaluate life.

Following ART, the client contacted me.

"The last time I was in touch with my family it was to say goodbye," the client said. "Today I invited them to join me to celebrate my new life."

CHILDREN

Trauma occurring in childhood deeply impacts identity and shapes beliefs about self and the world. Development is severely affected and can result in challenges across the lifespan.

We know that, even with the most diligent parenting and best intentions, children are vulnerable to trauma. Their trauma can arrive through direct experience or through witnessing an event. Childhood trauma is usually repetitive such as sexual, physical, or emotional abuse (which affects as many as one in seven children), or bullying (which can be just as damaging psychologically). It occurs during critical neuro-developmental periods and interferes with the development of a healthy stress response system; it compromises the child's future psychological, social, and emotional development.

Trauma in childhood can result from:

- physical, sexual, or psychological abuse; or neglect
- combinations of the above, including relating to trafficking
- violence and/or instability within the family
- violence and/or instability within the community
- sudden or violent loss of a loved one
- substance use disorder (personal or familial)
- refugee and war experiences (including torture)
- serious accidents or life-threatening illness for themselves or a family member
- stress related to being in a military family (deployment, parental loss, or injury)
- stress related to having a parent diagnosed with PTSD or C-PTSD (military or civilian)
- exposure to terrorism
- experiencing natural or man-made disaster
- dealing with the stress of having criminal or civil proceedings within the family with which the child is directly or indirectly involved
- living with an ongoing physical disability caused by neglect/violence/the actions of a perceived caregiver
- gender expression and 2SLGBTQI+ issues
- homelessness

- bullying.

Symptoms in children can manifest as depressive episodes, anxiety, difficulties with self-regulation, problems relating to others or forming attachments, regression, or loss of previously acquired skills, attention and academic difficulties, nightmares, difficulty sleeping and eating, and physical symptoms of pain, drug and/or alcohol use, risky behaviour, and participation in unhealthy sexual activity.

Of course, the impact on young children is huge because their sense of safety depends on the way the caregivers perceive their own. Early trauma in infants results in more dissociative symptoms. Trauma later in childhood leads to increased anger and emotional lability. Traumatized children experience the world differently, such as a child in class listening for signs of an impending verbal or physical attack.

Shockingly, according to SAMHSA, two thirds of children report experiencing at least one traumatic event by age sixteen.

THERAPISTS

You, as a therapist, are also a member of a specialized population that is both front-line and further down the line of urgent care for those who are affected by trauma. Sure, you may also be a single parent, a survivor of abuse, you could even be a therapist within the military — special populations overlap. Within that overlap, you may find yourself requiring therapy for events that happened in the past that have resurfaced, or you may experience a car accident, death of a loved one, or the diagnosis of an illness that is traumatic and takes you into personal trauma territory you've not experienced. Likewise, you may be affected by the work you are doing if there is not enough self-care established. Even with ART, a modality that is gentle on the therapist's career, pressure can build and combine career with personal life events — current and/or past — to be the proverbial straw on the camel's back.

QUESTIONS

List a few specialized populations that you've worked with that have not been mentioned here.

Give yourself a rating for your cultural competence — say, between one and five, where one is poor and five is excellent. And then honestly explain why you gave yourself that rating.

What are the most important things about specialized populations you'd like to remember when working through ART with your clients?

REFLECTIVE NOTES

CHAPTER 7

SELF CARE ~ THE COMPASSION CONNECTION

Trauma work is incredibly hard and complex work. Therapists can and do burn out quickly.

We all experience trauma in our lives, be it medical trauma, financial crises, divorce... we live complex lives. We are each a host for that trauma, providing an environment for it to exist. Sometimes it will thrive and manifest into severe symptoms designed to help us cope, and other times the host environment can process and evict it or find a place for it where it does not create havoc.

I have wanted to be a social worker since I was in grade eight. My adoptive mother said that I couldn't possibly be one because I was "too emotional."

She was wrong. Sadly, she misunderstood many things about me. I was not too emotional to be a social worker. I changed lives and, in my private practice, continue to change lives (including my own). My emotions allow me to do that. It is a gift. We must be vulnerable. We need to be vulnerable. For that is not only a strength, but also a superpower. It opens the doors and windows to progress and growth.

Which is not to say that trauma work doesn't put us at risk of suffering from trauma.

Your journey will comprise many paths; it will likely become more meaningful than you initially thought it would because of that which you experience. Then, that experience will become wisdom that will become mentorship and inspiration to others. You will bring ART to your communities and further develop them within your practice.

WHETHER YOU SUFFER TRAUMA FROM BEING EXPOSED TO TRAUMA IN YOUR WORK AS A THERAPIST, OR YOU HAVE EXPERIENCED YOUR OWN TRAUMA IN THE PAST, YOU MUST TAKE CARE OF THE CAREGIVER.

You have probably told many a client's loved one to do that. You are a caregiver too. In this final chapter of *Section II: You, the Therapist*, and before we move into *Section III: You and the Patient before ART*, I am compelled to call you to compassion (come, passion) and self-care.

Look out for your colleagues and yourself. Approach yourself as you might a beloved colleague. Recognize that by virtue of being a therapist, you are in a specialized population of a helping community. If you do require help, be sure to put yourself first. This means don't enter therapy for yourself with the idea that it'll be a great way to see the other side for your clients' sake. Be there for you first.

As professionals, we are required to do our own work if and when things come up. You have the perfect therapy right beside you — let ART work for you. While you can use the self-use eye-movement therapy on yourself to move sensations (as I do), I recommend for deeper work that you locate and engage an ART-trained therapist near you.

But there are other self-care practices that can stave off a trauma manifestation. Let's talk about those now.

COME, PASSION AND COMPASSION

Self-compassion is not simple to give nor accept. Such an embrace involves surrendering to fear, pain, the unknown, and requires the literal letting go of rejection, abandonment, security, and survival.

It is through the process of compassion — and it is a process — that compassion will be drawn to us, will arrive, and will enter then ignite the fireflies (the purpose) within each of us.

We all have passions. Through compassion we can encounter the purest form of energy. The creative energy of ultimate love.

To get to that point, to evolve to a compassionate agenda, we need to look at what is imbalanced in our lives. To truly examine what the blocks are. And that's where it becomes challenging because it is within the imbalance that our self-worth tends to be validated... externally.

When we do the work and identify the imbalance, and respond to it, then we will find ourselves journeying as far as we can in our physical form until that form cannot exist and the soul and spirit release as energy to continue to be a source of love, and a generational legacy of love.

To love and be loved is our purpose on this human journey called life. We are a life in process and a love in progress. Whether we like it or not, as humans we require balance, as we live in the duality of the human experience and our spiritual connection.

This is a deep concept. It can feel in direct opposition to the promotions, awards, degrees, and kudos we receive from others. There is nothing wrong with those wonderful *things*, as long as we live in the duality of knowing those *things* are not the source of our joy. They are simply external contributors.

REFLECTING ON YOUR HUMANITY AND VALUE

Compassion fatigue is the gradual lessening of compassion over time. Compassion stress is the demand for action to relieve the suffering of others. Self-compassion involves treating yourself with the same kindness, concern, and support you'd show a good friend.

Compassion for oneself is a tough sell to a helper of others. People in service to others might talk the talk of compassion and self-care — marking a massage on the first Saturday of each month, a once-a-week ice-cream sundae, or a cheeky hour reading a romance novel or a tawdry western in the back of a favourite coffee shop as self-care — they might even follow through with it. There is value to that, but that is only the self-care half of it (and only if it's followed through on). That talk is missing the self-compassion angle.

Compassion means to suffer with, and when you suffer with someone who needs a shoulder, an ear, a blanket, they feel a warmth that helps them believe that everything will be okay, that there is hope for them in their situation, that they are acknowledged. This is not to be confused with pity. Pity involves shame and is about perceived misfortune.

Compassion is understanding that suffering is part of a shared experience. It is a great equalizer in understanding that perfection means imperfection. In being imperfectly you, you are perfect.

Have you ever sat with yourself and exercised self-compassion at or after times you perceive you've failed, messed up, didn't understand, ran late, took on too much, became overwhelmed, broke down in tears, or second guessed your path in life?

Many carers, helpers, therapists, and first responders believe they are immune to needing help.

You may excel at providing compassion. You may see it as a weakness to receive compassion from others or from yourself. Some therapists feel they can't do their work if they identify as needing what their client's need; perhaps unprofessional.

Self-compassion involves acting the same way toward yourself as you do to others; to bring yourself comfort when you perceive you need it, or when you recognize there's something you don't like about yourself.

The flip side of self-compassion is being hard on yourself. Ask yourself how you comfort yourself; check in and examine if you use negative phrases like, get real, grow some balls, stand up straight, or even have that British phrase echo in your head: stiff upper lip.

No matter your level of understanding, challenge yourself at this moment by asking if you truly honour and accept your humanness. As a person who understands how to deliver ART, knowing that you are willing to serve your clients, are you willing to go to bat for yourself? Have you identified with some of the issues your clients bring forward, then told yourself that you are different because you're the therapist? Or you'll take care of you later? Or you're stronger than them, or it could be worse, so your stuff doesn't matter?

It is only when you open your heart to the reality that you are human too that you can stop fighting against the concept of self-compassion. You can still go to that massage every month, and grab that ice cream and read that silly novel, but you can do it knowing you are celebrating a wholly-cared-for self. That it is not an escape, but a true expression of your individuality, your preferences, your sense of fun, your deep love for yourself.

Self-care exercises can bring passion, reignite your passion, or raise your existing passion to a higher level.

You are a therapist, and you are human, and you are a first responder helping others heal from trauma. You deserve to be loved along with everyone else.

WHAT DO YOU NEED?

Dr. Chris Germer and Dr. Kristin Kneff are both well known in the field of mindfulness and self care. Their work has inspired many, including me.

To ask ourselves what we need, even when we don't know what we need, is a powerful exercise in self care. Being able to stop and recognize that we might need something different, to identify what that something is, and then taking action — well, it can be nothing short of profound.

Some years ago, I was at a conference in Ireland. The material was excellent but it was not resonating with me as I thought it should. I found myself somewhat critical of the delivery — perhaps then somewhat judgmental, thinking too much about the way I would do it and that it was not the way it was being done. I was distracted and, at first, I sat stirring that distraction as it burbled into annoyance. Late into the morning session, I stopped and blocked out what was being taught and I asked myself, *Colleen, what do you need right now?* Even though it took a few minutes to identify what I needed, just stopping to check in with myself, giving myself permission to articulate a want or a need, immediately I felt calmed. I was surprised when my self answered, *You need to go out and walk in the Irish countryside.* Who stands up to leave a session like this while in process? Apparently, me. I pushed away my papers, stood, and slipped out of class so as not to disturb the lecture. Then I walked, and walked, and walked. After a couple of hours, feeling soothed and refreshed, I returned to the course.

The facilitator asked me if I felt I had received what the self-care and mindfulness course was meant to be delivering. "Oh, yes," I said. "I understand and have received it perfectly — and I took it a literal step further and acted on it. I both understand and demonstrated what it is to care for self." I continued the rest of the sessions with a sense of joyful energy, recharged and better for having practiced what was preached.

ALTERING THE HARSH TALK

You can do this over several weeks. It will be the foundational plans for changing how you relate to yourself long-term. Journaling helps. Others are more comfortable doing via internal dialogue. Journaling is transformational. If you're inconsistent with paper and pen, use the recording feature on your phone to create a verbal journal.

1. Notice when you are self-critical. You might be so used to your voice that you are judging yourself and admonishing yourself most of the time. What words come up often, what phrases? And the tone of your voice: whose voice is it? Remind you of anyone?

Let's say you've been to the dark side — the ice cream — and had what you deem to be an excess amount. Let's say your self-talk was, "You're disgusting, you cow, you fat pig, you..."

Basically, pay attention to how you talk to yourself.

1. Try to soften that conversation with compassion. Talk to your inner critic in a respectful way, for example: "Hey critic, I know you're trying to keep me safe, but you do it in such a way that it's not helping. I don't appreciate your voice, your tone, your message."
2. Reframe the observations. Imagine the way a friend would speak to you with terms of endearment. "Dear, sweet one. Beautiful soul. Hey, beautiful one. I know you ate a container of ice cream because you're sad right now... you thought it would cheer you up, but it seems you're feeling even sadder. How about grabbing your sketch pad and drawing to feel better, or go for a walk and look at the river?"

When you reframe, you might wish to stroke your arm, or hold your face in your hands, or place your hand over your heart. Over time, once you act kindly, the true caring will flow.

THE JOURNAL OF SELF-COMPASSION FOR THE RECOVERING CRITIC

For one week, keep a daily journal of when you're hard on yourself. Use your paper calendar if you need to so you don't have to find another book. Review each day's events: did you judge yourself? Did you get annoyed at someone, make a rude remark, then feel ashamed and immediately judge yourself some more? Write about your emotions over the events. If you're stuck, use the prompts: I felt ashamed when... I judged myself when.... I was frightened when...

Work on *not* belittling your experience.

Next, write the ways that the experiences could have been connected to the larger human experience. For example: if you reacted angrily to something or someone, know that sometimes everyone overreacts. Forgive yourself and, without blaming, look at how you might have been on edge...

there was a lot of traffic and I started out late and didn't plan for a detour to my appointment after lunch.

Engage in self-kindness by writing some comfort words and resolving to know you can be extra patient to that person or let them know you were out of line.

By doing these three things in a journal format you will be able to work on changing your inner critic.

KEY DIFFERENCES

Recognize that self-compassion is not self-indulgence. It doesn't mean that you're going to grant yourself all kinds of permission to do wild things that go against healthy habits — self-indulgence is like eating a family-size container of ice cream. It is more like a conversation with a gentle and loving friend who wants the best from you; a meeting with your higher self, that sage or wise one you have inside.

Self-compassion is not self-esteem. Self-esteem is about self-worth, perceived value. Many times, self-esteem is based on perceived success or failure, rather than accepting that every choice, action, and outcome is a learning experience.

Self-compassion doesn't depend on external circumstances, rather it is knowing the self deserves understanding from the self. It's an inside job. It has nothing to do with competition or needing to be better than others. Self-compassion results in a powerful force of self-growth and change — all within a safe environment you prepare for yourself with self-love.

When we can recognize our own suffering, we can create a safe environment for ourselves, within ourselves. When you deliver ART, you are providing a therapy which is gentler on you in terms of the energy it demands of you. You are not a long-term caregiver for your clients (even though you are invested).

YOU ARE A LONG-TERM CAREGIVER FOR YOURSELF

Self-compassion involves self-care; engage in your expertise and bring it to yourself.

There is such a thing as the thriving therapist. You can thrive *and* make a difference in the lives of others who have great suffering. You have the key to help them through ART.

So, how *do* we teach ourself compassion, and how *do* we accept that compassion when we need to?

Here's how: develop a secure attachment with yourself and within yourself. No matter where you are and what might be going on in your life, you have the ability and capacity to self-soothe and not to numb out.

To self-soothe is to example secure attachment.

It doesn't matter if you have a family member who is pushing buttons to bring drama to the situation, or a friend melting down, or a spouse escalating a discussion with you... when you are securely attached you will remain aware, mature, and appropriate; less likely to regress to a specific developmental stage.

Invite compassion. Invite self-compassion.

COME, PASSION

Compassion, divide before my eyes so I can understand your
meaning.
Come passion.
Come, passion, come. Come sweep me off my feet.
Let me dance through your wide-open doors whose threshold
leads to the heart.
Transport me from fear...

Because:
Fear highlights illusions and obscures the path to truth.
Fear dampens all dreams, and in fear there is no freedom to create, to visualize, to move.
Come, passion.
Come to me because heartfelt compassion for the self is what anoints the re-awoken.
It is the covenant of our eternal existence.
Arrive at the door of my mind, body, and soul to show me that it is only when the process and experience of self-compassion is experienced, then recognized as the door to love, can we evolve past our human form and further integrate into our spiritual being-ness
Come, passion, come.
Compassion, bring your meaning so that through knowing you the world can be changed...
Because:
Not to have passion is not to live.
It means we miss joy and rapture — those elements released through passion, and that place from which we create miracles.
Not to have passion is not to have hope.
To miss the experience of absolute, exquisite love.
Come, passion, come. Bring along Hope to turn on the light.
That light within my centre that allows me to know an absolute, exquisite love that is the culmination of knowing, owning, and giving of the self.

— COLLEEN CLARK

QUESTIONS

This chapter's questions require awareness, honesty, and self-analysis.

What do you judge or criticize yourself for? (Appearance, job, relationships, parenting?)

What language do you use when you notice you've made a mistake?

How do you feel inside when you're being highly self-critical?

Do you feel cut off from others when you notice something you don't like about yourself or… do you feel connected with others (fellow humans who are also perfectly imperfect)?

Can you list the consequence(s) of being hard on yourself?

How might it feel if you could love and accept yourself as you are? (Does this scare you or give you hope or both?)

How do you treat yourself when challenges occur? Do you stop to comfort yourself or reassure yourself or ignore that you're suffering and go straight to fixing the issue? Are you carried away by the drama of the situation?

Most of us live in a world that does not emphasize self compassion. We believe we are lazy and indulgent if we don't give ourselves a harsh evaluation. We're told we're not good enough. Go over the cultural norms you've accepted into your sphere.

REFLECTIVE NOTES

SECTION III: YOU AND YOUR CLIENT BEFORE ART

CHAPTER 8

ESTABLISH A POSITIVE RELATIONSHIP

Every therapist/client relationship is unique in that it is based on an individual story — regardless of the categorization of trauma or commonality of symptoms which have arisen from that trauma. Often, for clients, the relationship with you will be the first close relationship they will have had for a long time; perhaps the first in which they disclose their deepest feelings and expose their secrets. Even in ART, where there is not as much talking as other therapies, the story is still there.

While you provide a safe place for a client's story, there will still be a fear of being judged or ridiculed. You are responsible to skillfully facilitate that safe place knowing that there can be an overwhelming urge for the client to cling to you as the only *friend* they've had, at least in the last while. There is an ideal space that you can provide which welcomes the client and does not cross the line of professionalism.

Therapeutic relationships must be unbiased, impartial, and transparent. It is not like an additional relationship formed with another professional, such as mechanic after they fix your car, because of a mutual interest in cars. Done right, an ideal therapeutic relationship is a safe place for you and your client.

LISTENING

Before you deliver ART to your clients, take the time to evaluate your listening skills, then hone them. Read, practice, consult experts, obtain a critique if you have any doubts about your listening skills — even if you have been in practice for a long time in your specialty.

PATIENCE AND PRESENCE

When you provide the time for a client to express themself — respect the pauses necessary for the client to answer a question, or for them to say "I'm ready for the next step" — then you are in a success zone. This involves patience. The very nature of how short ART timelines are compared to other modalities might tempt you to rush the process. Reflect on your timing of words, your speed of delivery, and your schedule outside of each client. Prepare yourself for those times when the client is not forthcoming. Check your habits such as watching the clock, tapping, shifting your body, altering your tone of voice, or daydreaming.

We all have responsibilities like running our home, laundry, family and friends, paying bills, picking up groceries, going to the dentist... the stuff of our daily lives. These can throw us off being present. When our clients, in the frantic-ness of their lives, struggle to meet their responsibilities, they don't need to sit before a mirror that is reflective of that chaos. Commit to being present in each session.

PREPARATION

Like the best Boy Scout or Smokey Bear, be prepared. Make sure you've gone over all the paperwork and files that have been transferred to you regarding your client.

WELCOME

Find the right way to welcome a client with calm body language, clear and even speech, and a pleasant environment. Inform the client of housekeeping issues, including bathroom location, water, tissues, and by stating the structure of the meeting up front so that there are no surprises — simple, but hugely impactful.

RESPECT FOR PRIVACY: YOURS AND THEIRS

Impartiality, being neutral, and privacy, form the foundation for a positive therapeutic relationship. Choose appropriate anecdotes to relationship build, make them feel at home, and allow them to understand they are not alone. Emphasize confidentiality in those anecdotes so that the client knows their unfolding story is protected too. A client will see and feel a well-balanced relationship as a result.

INFORMED CONSENT

Always make sure that if your client has any medical issues that they have a letter from their physician or their psychiatrist and know what medications they are on.

KEEP YOUR LANGUAGE SIMPLE

Your clients are not university students on their way to a Ph.D. in psychology; they likely do not work in that field. Establish the level — and decided on the tools — you will use to communicate concepts and stay consistent with them.

ALWAYS SET A POSITIVE STAGE

Spaces are important to me. They set the tone for the gathering. When I go into a conference room that I've rented for workshops and sessions, I have specific decorative props and snacks for attendees. I set the stage for positivity. This is not a chore or a ploy, but a genuine and heartfelt gesture to bring comfort and joy to our interactions and trainings. The items I incorporate say something about me and reflect my dedication. My private practice space reflects the same. What you do will speak volumes about you.

YOU ARE NOT FOR EVERYONE...

... and not everyone is for you. Be prepared to step in or out if it is evident that the relationship is not working. Be willing to refer if you are not the right fit for the client. Should this happen, adjust your solution and recommendations to align with the client's goals so as to avoid it coming across as rejection.

THE FEEDBACK THAT KEEPS YOU GOING...

When you receive feedback in the form of gratitude, you are on the right track. Use previous feedback to buoy new relationships.

This profession requires you be in a state of grace, holding space for others, taking responsibility for human lives seriously. It's soul work. Yes, others such as taxi drivers and retail salespeople can have high ethics and integrity around their profession, but people pay them — and tip them — and then go on their way. Your work is different than tapping a debit card and purchasing a product or service.

Not long ago, a person approached me in a public place. "Are you the Colleen Clark who is the therapist?" she asked. I nodded that I was, and this person continued to share with me that they had custody of one of their sibling's children early in life and that child had attended therapy with me in my private practice. The person was eager to share that the child had grown up to thrive, finishing university and getting a degree. They told me it was my kindness, from the start of the relationship, that was directly related to the success of the therapy.

"Your therapy has been powerful and effective on many levels," the person said. "That child, now an adult with a promising career ahead of them, still has the stuffed animal you gave them years ago."

As I thanked this person — tears in my eyes — and we began to part, they stopped and turned back to me.

"You saved that child's life."

When you are meeting your clients to provide therapy, meet them where they are, bring to the meeting those extras that will — through having done the assessment — be age and situation appropriate to creating a comfortable environment. A toy for a child. Flowers on a table for a gardener, a decorative file folder for a creative soul, a clean surface for someone who you know will appreciate attention to detail.

A COMMON PITFALL

Not all clients understand that their symptoms have developed as a response to their trauma. Clients *focus* on symptoms because the symptoms are creating the chaos. You might get caught up in that energy too. It is your responsibility to keep your client on track — and yourself — by delivering ART to deal with the trauma (not the drama). Clients need to know, up front, that once the trauma is dealt with, the symptoms stemming from that trauma can be worked via organizations like Alcoholics Anonymous, sessions with dieticians, or whatever is appropriate for that next stage.

The most positive relationships develop from you and your client being on the same page at the first meeting.

When you meet a new client in your workspace, you have already invested in that positive relationship. As you develop your new practice, or merge ART with your existing one, a checklist of what works for a positive start can help you keep track of necessary information.

As you learn about them, client by client, realization by realization, make notes. Gather your reflections for the building of your wisdom as a therapist, and as a humanitarian.

In the end you will have immersed yourself into your client's world.

EXERCISE

Review this personal story from my past and watch for areas where medical professionals did a good job of establishing a positive relationship, and where you think they fell down on the job.

In 2007, I experienced such a severe headache that I thought I might be having a stroke. I was taken to the hospital and stayed there for a couple of days, undergoing many tests. At that time, I was stable, therefore discharged. As I was at the front desk, fully expecting the staff to advise me my doctor would have some results by so-and-so date, a nurse casually said: "It wasn't a stroke, we found a brain tumour. We'll refer you to a specialist."

The delivery was so blunt, and the words so terrifying, I could hardly stand. My biggest fear had always been something happening to my brain.

I faced my own death in that moment, and then took life into my own hands... with a little help from timing.

The first thing I did was decide not to identify as my diagnosis.

The head of neurosurgery in a New York hospital suggested I meet with two doctors, one of whom was in Philadelphia. I took the redeye to Philly and spent the next day in consultation, being tested and learning about stereotactic surgery. When I returned to Calgary, I visited the doctor who'd diagnosed my brain tumour. "You might live until you're sixty-three," they said. Not once had they asked how I was doing psychosocially.

Later, post surgery, a health services organization asked me to write an article on stereotactic surgery from a patient's perspective.

When I had the procedure, a palliative care nurse — also a good friend — did Reiki on me during one of the procedures before the surgery. For the next nine months the swelling in my brain did not reduce. It became part of my life — a medical trauma.

Granted, I was an informed patient and able to surrender to the professionals I trusted. But the experience underscored for me the importance of medical and mental health professionals taking care to establish positive relationships with each patient.

QUESTIONS

From my story, above, where did the medical professionals do a good job of establishing a positive relationship with me? Where could they have done better?

How do you handle the start of your relationship with a client?

Have you found it difficult to fit all aspects into the first meeting, prior to the therapy starting? If yes, why? If no, why not?

Do you consider that initial consultation as part of the therapy?

How do you keep track of individual relationships in your practice?

Would you consider sharing your tips so that those who follow in your footsteps can create effective and best practices?

REFLECTIVE NOTES

CHAPTER 9

PROVIDE PSYCHO-EDUCATION

Psycho-education is evidence-based intervention delivered to clients, and those in their lives, which informs and supports them to better understand their situation and helps them cope with their illness. The delivery of information to the client is a game changer in therapy, and is a vital part of ART.

Practicing psycho-education provides you with the opportunity to have a strong relationship with your client and to normalize their behaviours.

PASSION TO EDUCATE AND LEARN

Educating your clients can lead to increased participation with treatment plans. When clients understand the diagnosis, they are more likely to view their diagnosis as treatable and remove the shame-component of it. Families are often involved in psycho-education components to assist in a whole-healing journey.

When clients understand — from well explained examples — that their symptoms are a natural response to trauma, their shame is reduced, and they can see that they are much stronger than they are fragile. Your dialogue with clients can include, "It makes sense why you'd have these blocks, so we're going to unblock them and then that will free up space. You might miss what filled up that space, yet it will be a new opportunity to put new things in that space. New thoughts, new behaviours, healthier ways."

Educating your clients is not always an easy task, since they are not always actively receptive due to their symptoms which were caused by underlying trauma. You must, therefore, take special care when providing psycho-education.

Your clients may believe they're broken. Educating them to understand their strengths, and that they have responded to trauma in a natural way, will clear a giant hurdle immediately. Think about the practice of Kintsugi... where the Japanese repair broken pottery with gold, thus making a more beautiful and unique piece. In ART we are taking the broken pieces and creating something solid and beautiful.

Psycho-education does not have to be provided at an academic level in a lecture. Anecdotes and examples are much more powerful. The education can be delivered in person at a consultation session, throughout therapy, and through handouts and videos.

You will need to provide psycho-education regarding some of the following topics for clients:

- Attachment and attachment patterns
- Impact of childhood abuse (physical, emotional, sexual abuse, domestic violence, etc.) and neglect in adulthood
- Loss and grief
- Mindfulness
- Mindful self-compassion

When a client has a thorough understanding of the methods that will be used for the challenges they face, specifically about the part they play in their own healing, they are better able to manage their journey in all therapies, be it the ART you deliver, or other modalities and programs they attend for their symptoms after you reset the amygdala via ART.

In general, you will want to transfer information about ART, as well as provide an overview of how trauma manifests in individuals, and how trauma — and the symptoms that arise from trauma — impact function.

You will know how to approach your client and what anecdotes and examples will work. Simple and relatable. Find the way to deliver the information that suits what you have learned in the assessment.

When you provide psycho-education, be sure to listen to your client's beliefs. Allow time for questions. List specific items that must be covered based on the information you've been given about them. Be sure to expand with some general information on the brain and brain function. Remember, as an educator not only are you teaching, but learning.

Build that therapeutic alliance by explaining what a therapeutic alliance is. Remind your clients that ART challenges traditional trainings. Explain that they will get into ART within the first two or three sessions once the assessment is done. Stress that you can move the trauma so that the brain has more space — due to the amygdala being calmed. Share concepts that have been covered in this book.

The window of tolerance concept helps us to think about our roles, and how we manage during stressful times. This neuro-scientific model illustrates the best *place* to be or the best state of arousal in which each of us can thrive. Imagine a river running through an open stretch of land, and the riverbanks being a bit precarious — a bit of chaos on either side of that river. On one side hyper-arousal, and on the other, hypo-arousal. Within the width of that river, we can manage ourselves — it's like we're in a zone of thriving, even when there are turns and the current is choppy. But if we move closer to the edges of the river — the riverbanks — or that wavy line each side of our zone of thriving, we can become hyper-aroused or hypo-aroused.

We each have our own window of tolerance which can change daily — within a reasonable range. The different width of our river, or thickness of our individual wavy line on the chart of ourselves, is due to factors such as significant childhood experiences, our neurobiology, social support, environment, and coping skills. The width of our river can vary, but the wider we can make it, the less likely we are to experience anger and frustration, or feel flat, low, and lacking in energy.

That which helps us remain in a state of thriving (in the river) varies, but in all cases that stimulus is basically run through the fight or flight response.

You are bound to have examples from your own studies and practices which you are overlaying as you read this book. Revisiting those examples that come to mind helps us remember how severe symptoms can be and how resilient humans are. When coping kicks in, in a normal response to stress, we witness our clients' pain and, as we practice delivery of ART to clients, we are able to see and record the relief, the healing, and the return to them being able to deal with symptoms. In recording reflective notes in a book such as this, the examples become teaching moments for those we mentor, and great refreshers for ourselves. We can see something different in those examples each time we go through them.

I encourage you to make a list of those cases you want to use as learning tools, as foundational anecdotes and case studies, and after the review that follows, feel free to purpose them into the reflective notes section. Think about the concept of how the body keeps score, and how you explain that to your client.

Customize your psycho-education component of your therapy. Interweave it into your sessions.

Imagine being able to be with a client and saying to them:

The body keeps score.
Your body has been keeping score.
I see you, I'm with you
and I'm moving these symptoms that your body is carrying.

Imagine asking them to close their eyes and to think about the lyrics to John Lennon's song, "Imagine." It is sublime, and peace-inducing. For you and for them.

The goal of therapy is to change the suffering into healing, and we do that through compassion. Ultimately, the alignment and joining with a client — the attunement, that psycho-education, the client needs — are a demonstration of *compassion*. They are the steps to compassion. To come to passion.

You have likely been, and will continue to be, the game changer in many people's lives. Your brand of care, tailored for each client, will allow them to learn and to heal. We all deserve to be heard and to be valued. Your words, the education you provide, and your stories will offer hope and be lessons of growth to your clients. When I am focussed on weaving the psycho-educational component into sessions, I will sprinkle stories from my professional life, threading them between delivery of fact-based, must-know, concepts and models within ART. Because psycho-education strives to inform and support, so that clients can better understand their situation, the use of an anecdote can not only support the client/therapist relationship but help you to put into perspective a psychological theory or concept. A key concept is inclusion and belonging; so many of our clients feel alienated from their peer groups.

Exploring a client's value system is an excellent way to help your client be present at the session. Their values may have shifted over time, but they will certainly have a belief system — even if it has been eroded.

CORE BELIEFS: BRINGING THE BASICS TO CLIENTS AND SELF

With your young clients, or those who you feel have shut down to the point of not knowing themselves anymore, going over core beliefs is a valuable exercise. It can work as a prerequisite to psycho-educational components.

Ask your client:

"What is your internal working model?"

"What is one of your negative core beliefs?"

Encourage them to dive deep and list three pieces of evidence contrary to their negative core belief.

GET DOWN TO BASICS WITH YOUR CLIENTS

Remind your client what a core belief is. Keep it simple.

Many people, not just clients, have negative core beliefs that cause harmful consequences. We are all human; therapists, celebrities, first responders, young, old... and we require self-assessment and self-care. To begin challenging negative core beliefs, first identify them:

Examples:

I'm unlovable
I'm stupid
I'm boring
I'm not good enough
I'm ugly
I'm worthless
I'm a bad person
I'm abnormal
I'm undeserving

YOUR VALUES

Be willing to evaluate your own core values as they apply to your personal life and your professional life. (This is a form of self-care.) Go over your own values and apply them to your journey to becoming a healer. Solicit the professional journeys of your peers, read biographies of others. Discover for interest's sake how they tick and use their stories to refuel yourself as well as refuel and renew them with yours. Some stories of being called to heal are phenomenal and even otherworldly; be careful not to discount any.

EXERCISE

I'd like you now to pay attention to the core values and negative beliefs that might be present in the following story from my past.

School was a wonderful relief from the chaos of my adoptive home. In grade six I joined the choir. I loved it. Never missed a practice. I was the little red-headed kid singing her heart out. At the season's end, the class was to go to the Kiwanis music festival at the Jubilee Auditorium — it was a big deal. Shortly before the festival my teacher came to speak to me. "Colleen," she said. "You can come to the festival but you will need to mouth the words." I didn't fully understand until she repeated herself. "Do not sing, Colleen. Pretend to sing." Her words destroyed me. I'd long been silenced at home and now I was silenced at school.

It wasn't until I went to Mount Royal College (it's been renamed and is now known as Mount Royal University) that I found my voice again. I remember my first day there: finding my classroom and taking a seat, listening to the instructor going over the values of social work. She spoke of self-determination, and how everyone has value. *Everyone has value.* I began to cry tears of joy and relief. I felt as if I had come home.

In grade six the teacher had told me I wasn't valued by telling me not to sing. My adoptive family had always made me feel I was not valued. Then, here I was at university and the instructor's words were golden. She continued with inspiration: "If you think you're an A student, you will be. If you believe you're a D, you will be." Thoughts determine who we are because they become our belief system. Those thoughts are often the voices of others.

I was valued, I would be an A student. I graduated with 3.96 grade point average.

QUESTIONS

In the above story, what negative core belief was present? Where did it originate? And how did it get resolved?

Your turn: what is your internal working model? What are your negative core beliefs? And then, list three pieces of evidence contrary to each negative core belief.

What areas of psycho-education do you feel it is important to cover with your client?

REFLECTIVE NOTES

CHAPTER 10
BUILD A DEVELOPMENTAL THEMOGRAM

Developmental wounds are at the heart of immature, anxious, or fearful clients and those who may be labelled resistant or fearful. It's highly likely that each client referred to you for ART has already been subject to psychometric testing and other specific assessments in order to receive their diagnosis. Those tests and assessments likely illuminated the deficits in the client's skill development and the skills they need to develop post ART. An ART treatment process oriented toward addressing your client's development deficits results in a more comprehensive resolution of their trauma.

DEVELOPMENTAL THEMOGRAM

A developmental themogram (my name for a genogram) is a tool that helps us, in our role as a therapist, to visualize the dynamics of family and other relationships and how they have been influenced in both the past and present. A themogram does a number of important things:

- provides the foundation for healing
- normalizes the sharing of deeply personal information at an early stage of therapy
- models to the client innate and expected capacity for self-regulation during sharing of information
- foreshadows the structure of the treatment plan
- suggests a causal and interruptible link between experience and current functioning
- looks at the relationships between family members across generations as well as important medical histories, and
- can uncover generational wounds that continue to strain relationships between family members, psychological factors, and hereditary patterns.

High-risk and high-needs clients share common patterns of unresolved early life negative experiences (infancy to adolescence) such as neglect, abandonment, abuse, loss, and trauma. Negative or suboptimal life experiences impact limbic-cortical structures, which in turn impact perceptual, emotional, and behavioural processes. They hamper the ability to address and complete tasks fundamental to normal developmental stages and compromising the achievement of maturational milestones.

You'll recall our discussion of Bowen's Family Systems Theory from Chapter 4, which suggests the family functions as an emotional unit. This means your client can be better assessed in association *with* their family unit rather than as an individual. Bowen's theory states that each family member is affected by and affects other family members. Balanced behaviour creates harmony, dysfunctional behaviour creates imbalance.

What follows is a visual example of a blank themogram template. In Chapter 11 I'll share a case study example and accompanying completed visual themogram.

THEMOGRAM TEMPLATE

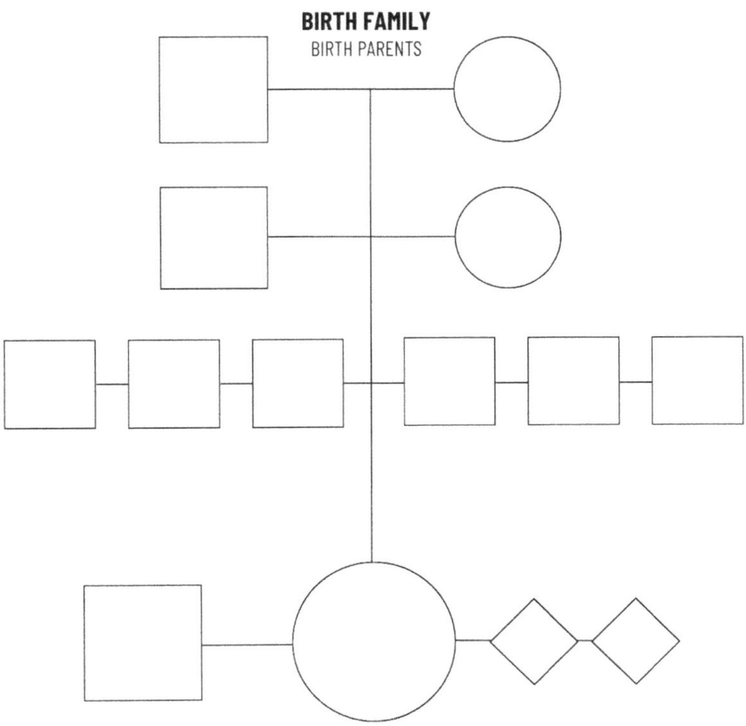

SYMBOLS

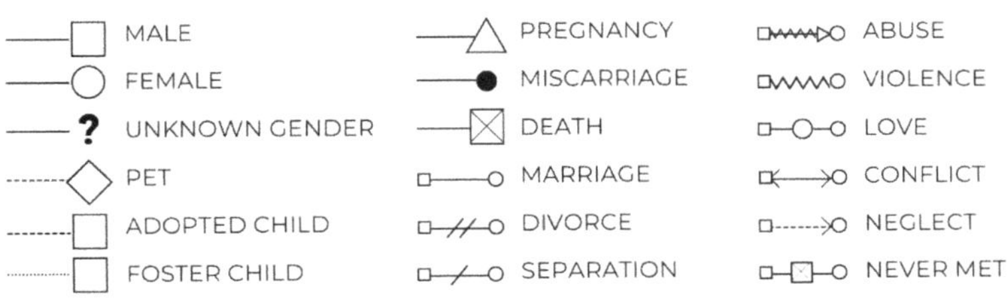

How you use a themogram will depend on each client and their circumstances, but here are some possibilities.

UNCOVER ROOT CAUSES

Even the closest family member may not know what has caused another member's behaviour. A child changes from being happy-go-lucky to sullen and their school performance drops. Why? The child probably can't explain it, and it won't be obvious to the parent(s). Perhaps there was a recent separation, and the parent left at home is adjusting to the new single-parent responsibilities. The resulting change in the parent's attitude is affecting the child's behaviour, When the child is invited to create a themogram, the cause of the behaviour change becomes obvious without the therapist having to force the child to talk directly to it.

PROMOTES UNDERSTANDING

Themograms help show us how a problem has evolved over time and how it continues to affect the whole family. The themogram can also introduce cognitive change as it cultivates insight, awareness, and promotes understanding of the cause(s) behind long-standing family problems. It can also foster greater empathy and intimacy as clients better understand what's behind their family's current challenges.

INITIATES BEHAVIOUR CHANGE

A themogram can help clients see the role their own attitudes and reactions are playing within troublesome family dynamics. This helps create a willingness to take ownership of their emotions and to at least begin to change their behaviour.

PAVES THE WAY FOR DISCUSSION OF DIFFICULT ISSUES

Drawing a themogram helps clients focus on drawing the themogram rather than the intense emotions generated from thinking or talking about the subject. This promotes feelings of being safe and opens the door to conversations about the issues.

HIGHLIGHTS STRENGTHS

A themogram also highlights the strengths in a family situation that will offer support for the client toward recovery from their trauma. It can also trigger new communication between family members, as there are bound to be questions that only another family member can answer.

HOW WE RESEARCH A DEVELOPMENTAL THEMOGRAM

Taking a comprehensive history and building the themogram should take a seventy-five-minute session (McGoldrick and Gerson and Ericksonian hypnotic language). You'll collect and then examine the following information:

- basic demographic details and structure of individual's family (grandparents, parents, siblings, children, stepchildren, adoption)
- family systems, family dynamics, large and small "T" trauma experiences
- contextual information (medical and therapy history, attachment, emotions, anger, gender, sexuality, romantic love, culture)
- developmentally interruptive experiences: witness or victims of domestic violence, physical, sexual, or emotional abuse and at what age, neglect, abandonment, separations (apprehensions, foster care, adoption, hospitalization, medical conditions or

surgeries, pregnancy traumas, moves or job losses, immigration, incarceration) disasters, school traumas, bullying, learning disabilities, religious abuse
- substance abuse, sexual addictions, eating disorders, dissociation, anger management, depression, suicide attempts or ideation and age started, homicide ideation and age started, personality disorder diagnosis
- current safety and safety factors, social support system, and physical support prior to ART
- loss, whether they are grieving, how they grieve
- is their grief traumatic grief (sudden, unexpected, violent, or complicated), disenfranchised grief (pet, miscarriage, grief over someone the griever no longer had a relationship with at time of death), or complicated grief (ongoing, heightened state of mourning, interrupting the ability to focus outside the grief).

OTHER QUESTIONS TO ASK YOUR CLIENTS

- When did you notice a shift or a change?
- How would you define moral injury?
- Have you ever numbed out? If yes, when was the first onset?
- When have you gone against your values?

Everyone's narrative will be different. You will need to get a feel for a client based on the population they belong to, and then develop your list based on the tenets of a special population. In the case of a first responder, perhaps a police officer, you'd want to know:

- their motivation for joining the organization (and if there is a family history of joiners)
- how many years they have served and how many transfers or postings

- the culture of their organization
- their values and beliefs and how those fit within the organization — constantly examine beliefs because it impacts our practice
- when they noticed changes in their perception of themselves and the world — what was the inflection point
- when they think other people noticed their change
- whether they have experienced a moral injury.

Knowing what's happening with the client who has been referred to you, in their lives, their day-to-day and their history, and without labeling them in one category, makes a significant difference in the results of their therapy. We'll discuss applying the discoveries from the themogram to your therapy plan in the next chapter.

STRATEGIC DEVELOPMENTAL MODEL (SDM)

A variation on my developmental themogram is the strategic developmental model (SDM), created by Maureen Kitchur in Canada in 1996. Kitchur created the model "out of desperation in the face of the overwhelming treatment needs of severe- and multiple-trauma victims, forensic clients, and short-term funded high-risk" clients. She describes it as a comprehensive and efficient method for delivery of maximum benefits of therapy when such therapy might be interrupted "by the realities of funding or of a multi-problem life." SDM:

- addresses or circumvents fear, hostility, anxiety, and resistance which often undermines or sabotages therapy with high-need and high-risk populations
- provides a systematic means of assessing and treating fundamental developmental causes of pathology and symptomatology to assist high-risk and high-need clients to break cycles and patterns of functioning

- encourages transference to facilitate reparative attachment and encourages deep attunement between client and therapist
- provides therapist with a structure for history-taking, assessment, and a developmental hypothesis which support formulation of a macro therapy plan
- contains sensitive, facilitative, flexible language that assures clients of their safety and rapidly engages both client's conscious and unconscious resources and cooperation, effectively using an Erikson healing trance. The client has increased ability to envision a positive outcome with a detached curiosity, developing belief in the possibility of healing, paradoxically leading to the desired outcome. Increased suggestibility allows client to align with a confident vision of healing
- offers flexibility in targeting strategies to meet the needs of diverse populations, children, teens, mandated or wary adults, recent trauma victims, PTSD; physically ill; repressed memory, fragmentary memory, or amnesia.

SDM helps therapists persuade, empower, and bring healing to a client's current symptoms. SDM avoids focussing on the problem or symptoms and instead seeks to interrupt the problem by resolving the developmental conditions that have been perpetuating the problem and the symptoms. It uses strategic language to bypass resistance and facilitate rapid progress — language specifically designed to strengthen ego, support resourcefulness, and honour the individual. The central strategy of SDM leads clients to heightened levels of self-esteem and a sense of integrity/wholeness — without depersonalizing, mystifying, or confusing the client. Therapeutic outcomes of self-esteem, integrity, and wholeness are equally important to the resolution of the problem.

SDM does not require a client's young ego states to show up to a session because the therapeutic tasks of each stage of therapy are age appropriate — younger ego states can be healed prior to the client engaging in later adult trauma work. SDM removes the need for lengthy resource installation or ego strengthening in ego-compromised clients such as survivors of severe sexual abuse and multiple childhood traumas.

It offers an alternative approach to doing simple chronological targeting of traumas. It often clears the developmental path, resulting in faster or more comprehensive resolution of all other targets and presenting problems. In psychologically older clients, SDM has been found to shrink or eliminate primary and secondary symptoms even before they have been directly targeted.

An attuned therapeutic relationship is at the core of SDM. Attunement behaviours are likely to assist in developing positive corrective attachment. Messages will go into the right part of the brain so that psychological and neurobiological developmental recapitalization occurs.

EXERCISE: CREATE A GENOGRAM FROM THIS STORY

Creating a developmental themogram is a more complex undertaking than this exercise allows. Still, I want you to have the opportunity to practice the way of thinking that will help you build themograms with your clients as you prepare to deliver ART. With that said, review this story from my past, and as you read, consider the elements that would inform a themogram if you were tasked with developing one with me.

HOMECOMING, HOMELEAVING

There have been many homecomings in my life — geographical places where the physical aspects of the landscape caused a brilliant sun to rise in me; emotional places that have filled voids in me that I had no idea were empty. Unexpected arrivals in indescribable lands — a state of heart, perhaps — where intuition met intellect and created an explosion of breakthroughs which could serve others. I say serve others, when I know that we collaborate to serve each other and ourselves because we are all connected. One person's breakthrough is also yours, and the story of their loved ones. We're all in this together. I experience them with clients as they come home to self through the healing ART provides.

Homecomings seem to be a way of life for me; I will feel a call to go somewhere and, when I arrive, I feel that I am home. I was adopted as a child; therefore I had a home-leaving not long after I was born.

A curious child, I recall being a pre-schooler and asking the Universe, God, or a Higher Power how I got here, and how I fit into this planet. I was pulled at a young age to the United Kingdom, and to other places. It was much more than an insecure attachment, which I do acknowledge given I wasn't sure where I belonged because I was adopted and did not have the opportunity to have a secure attachment with my birthmother, nor was my adoptive mother or family able to offer security to me.

Yet there was a spirituality about me or within me.

Spirituality is a highly charged word that can represent so much: belief systems, tranquility, nature, God, and all the above. We can recognize the importance of this concept for our clients as well as ourselves. Some will find that they identify with a strong spiritual self, others will not want to participate in any discussions where there's a whiff of spirituality involved.

When I was four years old — I would go to Sunday school by myself. My adoptive parents never took me. The closest church to our home was a Lutheran church. I somehow surrendered my life to a higher power, and I knew I would be of service in the future. I can't remember when I learned the meaning of my name, but Colleen means *girl* and Elizabeth means *child of God*. I knitted together all the information I had so far in my young, big-but-little life. I knew there was a purpose.

When I was six years old, I started piano lessons. One day I played "My Bonnie Lies Over the Ocean." The music was so incredibly powerful that it reached into my heart and aligned with meaning that was already there. Later, I learned that my birth family was from England and Scotland. Later still, I named one of my daughters Bonnie.

Throughout my life, I have felt the need to visit places that I strongly believed had been a part of my past. Peru was one of those places, as was Hawaii, and England. Each of these places gave me the feeling of being home.

As an adult, I learned about my birth family, and I met my grandfather on my father's side; he was from Glasgow. My maternal grandfather came to Canada in the early 1900s and initially joined the Royal Canadian Mounted Police. It was a story filled with trauma. He was a powerful man and, sadly, a cruel individual. He had his wife committed to an institution. When their daughter (my birthmother) became pregnant at sixteen years old, she knew her father's power and anger. She and my seventeen-year-old birthfather took a bus to another city to escape the tyrant. But her father intervened and sent my birthmother to a convent, and had my birthfather temporarily jailed. He then threatened my birthfather that, if he did not leave Alberta, something bad would happen. My birthfather then joined the navy. I later discovered he wrote many times to my birthmother, but his mail was intercepted, and she was told that he had taken his own life.

When she gave birth to me, she never saw me. I was swept away from her, and my adoption arranged by someone the doctor knew. It was a twisted mess of a situation. I was my adoptive mother's birthday gift. She had many issues, including anxiety, and my adoptive father was an alcoholic.

Life continued to weave its threads of connection through my childhood. I learned that my biological grandmother lived in the same city and had watched a little girl skate on the community rink — that little girl was me.

One evening, many years later, when I was on a child protection team, we were chatting as work colleagues do. My partner asked me, if I had a wish, what would I wish for. I think I surprised them. My answer wasn't a million dollars or world peace. I simply said that I'd like to find and meet my birthmother.

Two days later, my world exploded. My colleague said to me: "Colleen, I found your birthmother."

When I'd digested the information, there was phone contact, then I flew to Edmonton to meet her; the flight was like a journey through a birth canal. When we met it was uncanny to see we had the same gold jewellery. I discovered she was a classical pianist — I'd been called to piano lessons as a young child in my adoptive home.

After my birth, and after she'd been told my birthfather had died by suicide (which he hadn't), she had attended the Royal Conservatory of Music and dedicated herself to her music.

At the time, I was attending school for my master's degree and working full time. I decided I'd switch the subject of my thesis from interviewing sexual abuse victims (children) to the subject of adoption reunification and coming home to self. I became licensed as an adoption search agent.

I managed to find my birthfather's brother and discovered my birthfather had died years earlier. He'd been an artist. I received letters in which he asked about my birthmother and me. I worked on closure by visiting his grave in Victoria.

Through my life, I have come to accept all parts of my past, and I have compassion for both my birth and adoptive families — and for myself.

QUESTIONS

What do you still need to ask in order to complete the themogram based on this story from my past?

When we visit our history and journal or think about days gone by, we are essentially filling in a themogram for ourselves and being reminded of the milestones in our lives. What does your own personal themogram look like?

REFLECTIVE NOTES

CHAPTER 11

STRATEGIC THEMOGRAM

CASE STUDY

Let's now take a look at a case example and the corresponding completed themogram. The case example you'll read below is a work of fiction and not reflective of any one specific case, for confidentiality purposes. I have developed this fictional scenario for the sole purpose of demonstrating the process of conducting a client assessment and creating the themogram so that you can move on to identify themes and scenes and then ART can commence.

Meet my fictional Lucy B. She was referred to me after being diagnosed with PTSD, anxiety, and depression by her psychiatrist. The psychiatrist also diagnosed Lucy B. with complex trauma stemming from multiple events. In my example exploration of Lucy, I considered whether she might present with a history of events such as interpersonal threats during childhood or adolescence, abuse, neglect, interpersonal violence, community violence, racism, discrimination, or war.

CASE STUDY SAMPLE: LUCY B

Referral Notes from Psychiatrist

Lucy B. is a forty-eight-year-old indigenous female, widowed, recently on medical leave from a law enforcement agency. She joined the agency when she was nineteen years old. For the past five years she has been staff sergeant in an isolated rural posting.

Recently, Lucy was involved in a homicide/suicide investigation involving the death of a five-year-old girl. This traumatic event activated flashbacks, nightmares, hyper-vigilance, and avoidance. Lucy admitted to suicide ideation and to having a sense of hopelessness for the future.

Throughout her law enforcement career, Lucy had excelled as a female member within the organization. She's had fifteen moves in her twenty-seven-years with the organization. Some postings have involved very isolated locations (similar to the current posting). She has worked in child abuse, homicide, undercover, traffic reconstruction, and intelligence. She has experienced cases involving severe child abuse, ritual abuse, suicides, homicides, domestic violence, traffic fatalities, being victim of near-fatal shootings and witnessing her partner get shot, attending autopsies, natural disasters including forest fires, floods, and COVID-19. Her undercover work involved severe stress on her personal life and values, and exposed her to extreme risk as she infiltrated a national gang for human trafficking and drugs.

She describes experiencing severe bullying and moral injury within the organization and that due to the ongoing and systemic discrimination against women in the organization she felt she needed to keep quiet (not speak out or speak up) and to prove herself to others.

This is her first mental health assessment with recommendations for treatment. Lucy reported being worried and anxious about the meeting with the psychiatrist, believing the problem was "her weakness of not being strong enough" to deal with regular work-related events, which were really untreated OSI (operational stress injuries).

REVIEW OF KEY CONTEXTUAL EVENTS

This writer read the psychiatrist's complete assessments and made notes and questions in preparation for the developmental strategic themogram with specific application to ART.

Areas to explore:

— Father's and mother's history (step-parents, adoptive parents, birthparents); attachment patterns, and relational dynamics
— Roles in family of origin (and how these past roles shaped and impacted her life regarding patterns, habits, decisions and behaviours today)
— Losses (pregnancy, miscarriages, still births, infertility, pets, etc.)
— Number of moves in childhood and adulthood
— Foster care, adoption
— Bullying, domestic violence
— Suicide ideation and suicide attempts
— Neglect
— Relevant medical history
— Therapy history
— Addictions (age at onset and current usage): substance abuse history including pornography, gaming, etc.
— Eating disorders
— Medication history and current medications

ACTION TAKEN

This writer met with Lucy B. in private practice for four sessions prior to commencing ART. *(For a summary description of these first sessions refer to item five in the Resources section at the end of this book.)* During session four we completed the developmental strategic themogram, including identification of operational stress injury, and went further to identify themes and scenes.

This writer explained the rationale and purpose of gathering comprehensive information regarding her family of origin, which involved relationships, attachments, resiliency, losses, patterns, and potential trauma events.

Lucy B. is indigenous and became a permanent ward of the state and was placed in foster care when she was two years old. She has little or no memory of her birth family, her indigenous roots, or of her time in foster care. She has had no contact with any of these parties.

Lucy was adopted into a caucasian family at the age of four and was the youngest of four children in the home. The family moved at least six times, as her adoptive family was transferred to different communities. She was shy and quiet and had few friends due to the moves.

Her adoptive father was often travelling as a sales rep, away for weeks at a time. He had a drinking problem. Her mother was anxious and stayed at home. She saw little affection between her mother and father, remembers them fighting and hearing her mother scream. She often felt scared. To escape she'd create stories in her mind and be with the family dog, Lucky. One night her adoptive father took the shotgun and threatened to shoot her mother, the family, and himself.

She was told they wanted to adopt her because they had three boys and always wanted a girl. Lucy B. recalled one of the most significant losses of her life was when she was ten years old and her dog was euthanized. She didn't learn what happened until years later.

She recalls being sexually abused for four years (starting at age six until age ten) by her eldest adoptive brother, eight years older. She tried to tell her adoptive mother, who wouldn't believe her. The abuse stopped when the brother got a girlfriend. Lucy describes low self-esteem growing up. She has no contact with her adoptive family, except an adoptive brother who is two years older.

She was raised in the church (her adoptive mother's upbringing), finding a sense of belonging and connection with the church including a specific priest. Her faith continued to be a strength for her throughout her life. She stated she was considering becoming either a nun or a police officer when she was seventeen years of age.

Lucy's motivation to join law enforcement was to "help, serve, and protect the vulnerable." She has always been pulled to ingenious communities near her postings to search for her roots, but has not pursued.

At nineteen, she met another law enforcement member at training. They married when she was twenty. She describes this as the happiest time of her life. They built a home together and were looking to start a family. Then when she was twenty-four and her husband twenty-six, he was killed while on duty. She felt like she lost the only family she'd ever had, and that since then she's had no interest in any personal or intimate relationships.

The bullying she was subject to in the organization began once her husband died. She felt betrayed by the organization, more isolated, working twelve- to fourteen-hour days. During this time she developed an eating disorder. She described feeling numbed out. She held specific high-risk work roles, for example undercover, and wondered if she was passively suicidal.

Lucy B. saw her promotions as "proving to herself and others that she could do a good job." She identified that when another female member was reporting to Lucy a complaint against another member, she witnessed the organization not support the complainant. And Lucy suffered a significant moral injury as she was the one who had to tell the complainant that her concerns were considered "unfounded."

Lucy sought her current posting as a way to get back to a rural detachment where she felt she would be able to provide her expertise. She reported she has been established in the small community and has little or no connection with any family or friends. She reported that her dog, Mindy (age five) is her constant companion and that she continues to attend church.

She describes her eating disorder (bulimia) has increased since the latest OSI incident of the child/homicide and suicide. It was a custody case, where she was called after the non-custodial parent failed to return the child at the court-ordered specified time. Lucy was first at the scene.

Hence the referral to the psychiatrist and to me for treatment.

What follows is the themogram created with the information gathered during that fourth session with Lucy B.

THEMOGRAM SAMPLE

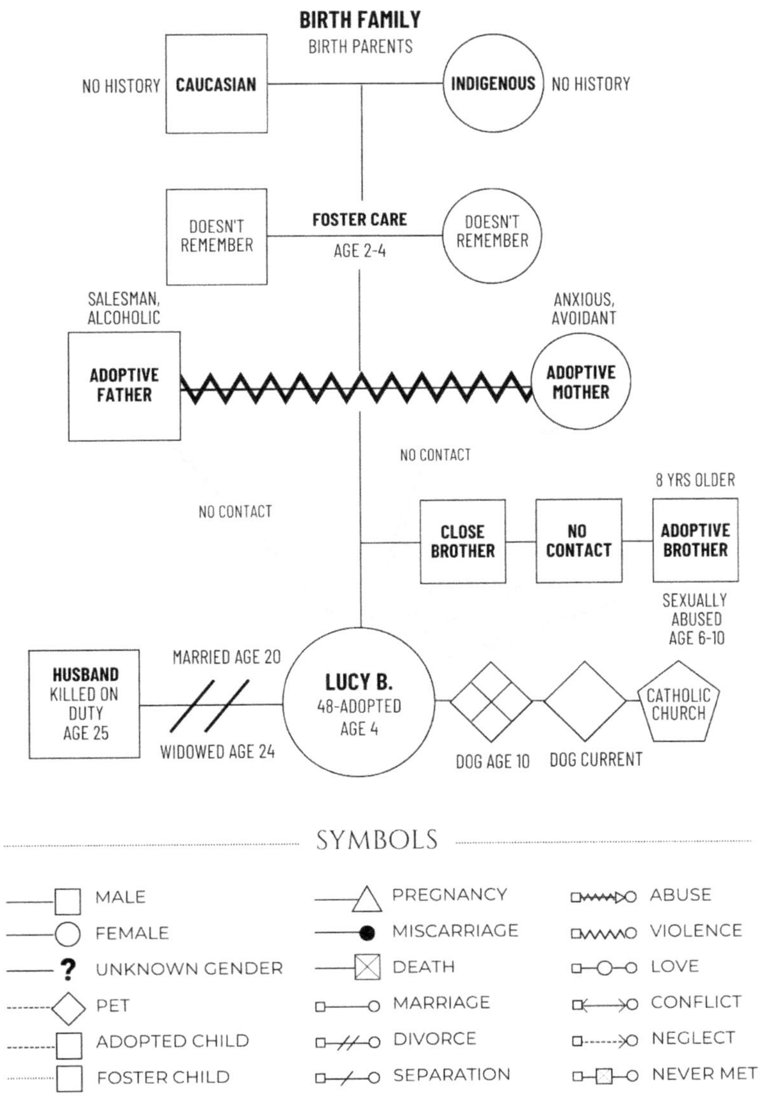

With my themogram for Lucy done, I would next turn my attention to developing the themes and scenes list to support ART. But first, before I reveal the themes for my fictional Lucy B., let's dive deeper into the process of developing themes.

QUESTIONS

Is there anything you would add or change on Lucy B.'s themogram based on my notes from those four pre-ART sessions? If so, note them here.

REFLECTIVE NOTES

CHAPTER 12
IDENTIFY THEMES

"*Who is my client?*" You'll have the answer to this question once you've completed your assessment and themogram. Now it's time to further conceptualize your client's world and experience. To do this, you'll want to identify themes, develop scenes based on those themes, and collaborate with your client to establish which theme to work on first.

A theme is a central topic, subject, or message. In a book, a story's thematic concept is established by the writer, and when it's done well it becomes what each reader thinks the work is about. It's similar in ART. The stories told to you by your clients become themes—subject matter, issues, overall concepts — regarding the life of the client.

DEVELOPMENTAL STRATEGIC THEMES FOR INTERPERSONAL AND EXTERNAL TRAUMA

- Neglect/attachment (identify primary attachment type)
- First thoughts of suicide (age); first suicide attempts (earliest and most recent method)

- Mental illness of parent
- Sexual abuse (most recent and earliest); any unwanted sexual contact
- Physical abuse (most recent and earliest)
- Emotional abuse (most recent and earliest)
- Domestic violence (witnessing age; and most recent —witnessing or receiving DV), physical, sexual, financial, spiritual, cultural, psychological
- Bullying (most recent and earliest)
- Loss and grief (traumatic grief; disenfranchised grief)
- Loss due to homicide and or suicide
- Historical trauma: colonization and the residential school experience of forcible removal from the family home; destruction of culture and language; adoption; child welfare
- Torture, forcible confinement, ritual abuse
- Elder abuse: physical, sexual, financial, spiritual, cultural, psychological
- Medical trauma
- Moral injury
- Divorce, separation, moves
- Being a victim of crime
- Sudden death of loved one (suicide, homicide, accidental, medical)
- Sudden and unexpected loss of a job, housing
- Living in extreme poverty
- Natural disasters (fires, floods, COVID-19 pandemic)
- Accidents; vehicle, plane
- Terrorism
- Immigration

These themes are then used to establish the route of the therapy and from which you'll create scenes.

On stage a scene is a small piece of the larger story played out to an audience. It is representative of something memorable and impactful relating to the theme.

In ART, you'll help your client choose a scene from their memory that best represents each significant theme. A scene can be a particular experience or an action taken against them, within the identified theme on which you are working together, and one that evokes the most emotion. Bringing out, reworking, and rewriting disturbing memories that are stored in the brain is key to stopping the triggering of intense emotions and physical reactions.

Examples of scenes can be:

- When a teacher admonished the client, as a child, in front of a class full of students
- When the client was assaulted in college
- A memory of coming home from school to parents who were unable to provide care
- A diagnosis of a medical condition — and that moment in the doctor's office, and afterwards the breakdown in the car when realization set in

ROADMAP OF HOPE

Your client's perceptions are usually highly relevant. I often invite the client to think about their world before the trauma — to externalize it. I use a whiteboard and ask them to illustrate that view. For example, I'll ask them to draw how they saw their world before their first responder work. When we can get our clients to identify a world before trauma and see it as a safe place, they will feel and see the shift as to how they see themselves in the world now. Next I'll ask them to draw how they would *like* to see it in the future. Then I ask them to illustrate how they saw the world after the trauma.

The whiteboard images become a roadmap — a roadmap that goes back to the starting point and then continues out to the future, bookending hope with hope. I want to know, and I want them to know, where they were pre-trauma in their cognitive functioning, then I want us both to know where they are now in the trauma, and finally where they want to be.

Ask: "How would you like to see yourself after therapy?" They might answer with: "I'd like to feel safe," or, "I'd like to have a boyfriend," or "I'd like to walk down the street and not be afraid."

At this point, explain that this is the roadmap. Assure them, "This is where we're going to go. Because we've got this. And we will get there." Have the clients take pictures of those notes: their life before the trauma, after the trauma, and how they want the future to look.

Once you understand their internal working model, then you can understand their landscape. You will be articulating something that is uniquely their experience and lead them to places they have never been. Ask them: "When did things change for you?" Gently guide and get them to affirm this powerful statement:

"It's not me, it's what happened to me."

My brain gathers material like a matrix; it puts together all the pieces of the internal workings of my clients — a model of the way their life is lived and experienced. Go as far as googling locations to familiarize yourself with landmarks familiar to them. Take the time to learn something culturally significant or educate yourself if the nature of their trauma was covered by the media.

Gathering the information may be like work you've done before — use your magic, your proven processes, because you know how you work best. Review the resources I've provided at the end of this book — I recommend you use them even if it feels unnatural to you.

The number of themes a client presents with can tie into your estimate of the potential number of ART sessions required. If a client has eight themes, they might have max of eight sessions; however, ART can generalize quickly and those might overlap.

Based on the themes and scenes I identify with my fictional case example for Lucy B., there may be as many as ten ART sessions for her. However, after each session I would evaluate the remaining themes. As you know, ART can generalize and we may be able to reduce the number of ART sessions.

LUCY B.'S CASE EXAMPLE THEMES

You've seen the themogram from my case example for Lucy B. Now I'll share with you my approach for developing the themes that would be the foundation of our theoretical ART work together.

Several of the themes I'd identify for Lucy B. relate to her job and role as a police officer. I'll group those together for you first:

- Homicide and suicide involving children. The scene would be the one Lucy B. attended to as an officer. This is the most distressing for her at this time, with flashbacks, nightmares, etc. It is also most likely connected to the time her adoptive father threatened to shoot and kill her adoptive mother, all their children, and himself. I won't be surprised if there is a scene match.
- Policing/child abuse, policing/undercover, policing/traffic: I'd ask Lucy B. to identify the most intense scene in each category and we would process that during ART.

Here are the other themes and scenes I identified:

- Loss and grief. The death of her husband would be processed as a scene. Scene matches would likely arise around other losses — pets, family members, colleagues.
- Apprehension/foster care/adoption themes regarding identity, abandonment, and rejection.
- Moral injury, related to incest and the policing organization in that situations were disclosed, but she wasn't protected. I would ask Lucy B. which scene is the most distressing and process.

- Bullying, related to both the policing organization and her childhood. Again, I'd ask Lucy B. which seems most distressing.
- Emotional neglect, with respect to childhood attachment. I'd explore with Lucy B. when she first noticed feeling numbed out and I would process that as a scene.
- Eating disorder. I would ask when she first became bulimic and process what the scene was. I would then be able to do ART *Typical Day* (the script referenced earlier and that you would have received in your ART training) for the eating disorder.
- Resiliency factors would include her faith in the Catholic Church and the strong attachment relationship she had with the priest in her childhood, the one with her husband, her adoptive brother, her childhood dog and her current dog.

At the end of the first ART session with Lucy B., I would also remember to teach her how to do self-use eye movements to manage negative sessions and to help her fall asleep at night.

My key for Lucy B.'s themogram, my list of themes could also look like this:

CHILDHOOD THEMES

- Sexual abuse-incest
  - Not protected
- Attachment
  - Anxious avoidant
  - Neglect
- Alcoholic family system
- Bullying school
- Being adopted (family of origin)
- Foster care

KEY: Lucy B.

- Apprehended age 2/foster care 2-4 (abandonment issues)
- Adopted age 4
- Domestic violence/adopted parents (gun threat)
- Sexually abused – adoptive brother ages 6 – 10
  - Disclosed adoptive mother, not protected
- Alcoholic family
- Attachment patterns – anxious/avoidant
- Loss, grief – death of dog childhood – primary attachment figure
- Numerous moves childhood – limited friends
- Connected to church/priest – resiliency
- Eating disorder – bulimia age 12
- Emotional neglect

**start with current index theme ART – homicide/child Suicide (connected to childhood)*

1 Current Index trauma – child/suicide homicide

First Responder / Law Enforcement Themes

- Homicide/suicide

*start scene child homicide/suicide (connected to adoptive father threatening to shoot family)

Themes

- Undercover – identify most intense scene
- Death / husband scene (losses family)
- Child abuse – identify most intense scene
- Traffic fatalities – most intense
- Moral injury – work
- Bullying – work

First Responder age 19 - 48

- Moral Injury
- Bullying
- Eating disorder
- Loss & grief

- Create – belong to a family
- Married age 20 to a colleague
- Widow age 24 (husband killed on duty)
- Numerous moves organization
- Numbed out – workaholic
- No relationships
- No children
- Close dog
- Bullied organization
- Positions – high risk – undercover
- Child abuse
- Homicide – suicide
- Traffic
- Still connected to church

DEVELOP AN ART THEME DOCUMENT

When you identify the themes, go into the most current, the most upsetting event out of, say, ten — or to the earliest your client remembers.

The specific themes will emerge as the root of the trauma. Lean on your ART training — the themes will indicate potential scene matches that may come up in ART processing. Follow *Typical Day*, the evidence-based ART script you received in your training, and do not deviate from it.

Between sessions, provide psycho-education, skill building, and even build in an integration session, but always move the trauma first, then use *Typical Day* for other co-morbidities (addictions, anxiety, depression, eating disorders, OCD, pain, etc.).

APPLYING THEMOGRAM/THEMES/SCENES TO THERAPY PLAN

Once you have your themogram and your themes/scenes list for your client, you'll move forward to create your ART plan as follows:

- Establish rationale: provide baseline information for any potential ART scene matches
- Developmental catch-up: minimization of resistance, maximization of safety and efficiency
- Developmental baseline: when all major developmental and trauma targets are numbered on themogram in chronological order of development. These are the core events to be ART-processed first. (Other presenting problems or symptoms might also be cleared through this process.)
- Identify parent and parent/child relationships
- Go to the middle-childhood (ages four to eleven) scenes, a concrete trauma timeframe, and negative memories of family-or-origin relationships; then go to adolescence and adult scenes including family relationships and traumas.
- Be aware of attachment wounds for personality disorders: narcissistic, borderline, anti-social, dissociative identity disorder (DID)

When working with complex trauma, I often start with neglect because that helps the client move developmentally. Whether or not that is the case with your client, establish your list of targets: developmental catch up; minimization of resistance, safety, and efficiency.

All client themes, scenes, symptoms, or issues are now placed on a re-assessment list to be reviewed after targets are cleared.

Here's the order in which to target parent and parent/child relationships:

1. Middle-childhood targets (four to eleven) are usually first. Known/identified trauma timeframes are targeted, as are concrete, tangible negative memories of family-of-origin relationships.
2. Early, preverbal childhood targets to process (O'Shea model)
3. Adolescent targets
4. Adult targets including family relationships and traumas.

Be aware of attachment wounds and watch for evidence of personality disorders like narcissistic, borderline, antisocial disorders.

ALL THE WORLD'S A STAGE

It's like Shakespeare's line in *As You Like It*: "All the world's a stage, and all the men and women merely players." I always imagine that stage under bright lights, with a celebratory, appreciative audience applauding the performers. There's an element of joy to it all.

In the case of clients with operational stress injury, trauma, and other mental health issues, their stage is often poorly lit or even in complete darkness. It's like someone has cut off the electricity, taken away the script, and all the supporting actors and staff have left the building.

ART brings that script back to them, and has them contribute to it. Clients become full participants: the star, the lighting manager, the playwright, the director, the producer... all under the guidance of you, the therapist.

QUESTIONS

What do you think is the biggest advantage to developing themes for the delivery of ART?

Have you developed themes when using other methodologies or modalities? If yes, how did they help? If no, what are the ways you think they can help in both ART and other therapies?

REFLECTIVE NOTES

REFLECTIVE NOTES

CHAPTER 13
EXPLAIN ART

Your client has likely been through trials and tribulations on their healing journey, thrust into meetings required of them by insurance providers or employee programs. There may even be a trail of failed attempts at therapy, and they've potentially languished on one or more waiting lists. Whatever their circumstance: fearful, hopeful, doubtful, tired, all the above, they will be looking to you for answers and help.

Your client may also be involved in legal or other processes perhaps related to the source of their trauma. If they are working with a lawyer, be sure to let them know they may require permission from the lawyer to proceed with ART. This is because in some cases, there is witness value in your client's emotional state while providing testimony. Once they complete ART, the processing of the trauma results in the retention of the facts of the trauma but not the emotional responses that arise. In this way, it may impact their value as a witness. It may sound cruel, but because the assessment of the victim impact affects judgements and outcomes, it may be determined that your client needs to delay their therapy.

Your client needs to understand what ART is and what their ART journey is going to entail. They need to know what to expect and to feel trust in the therapy model. They might even benefit from knowing a little of your story, but we'll get to that.

Your client is not your student in a university course, nor are they your protégé or intern. Meet them where they are. Create a professional yet comfortable explanation and space that respects their state of mind and level of comprehension.

START YOUR EXPLANATION WITH CREDIBILITY

Your client chose you or was directed to you because of your professional reputation, and that of your employer, agency, or association.

Introduce the fact that SAMHSA, in the United States, accredited ART.

It's great to have a checklist of points to make for speaking to clients about ART — I've provided one for you in *Section V: Resources* at the end. Firstly, though, as simple as this may sound to you, be clear what the letters stand for: Accelerated Resolution Therapy.

I will often weave my professional stories into describing ART — I bring it into a consultation script that informs the client right from the start so that they can decide if we are a fit and if the therapy seems right for them.

Creating a script of introduction can serve more than one purpose and cover more than one topic. I will include mine as the next chapter.

Make sure they understand the focus of the therapy: healing the developmental interruptions and traumatic experiences that have blocked access to those resources, and once that is accomplished, the second phase of therapy is to teach skills or fine-tune skills which they may not have developed.

EYE MOVEMENT

When you explain ART, talk about attunement and how the eye movements will create new connections with existing information in the brain. Share that ART works in the subconscious and the right side of the brain, and the limbic system. Get into explaining how ART significantly impacts the amygdala which allows for a reset through the movements and script. Get into the trauma-first focus.

They'll need to know the sessions of eye movements are brief. Emphasize that ART is not hypnosis. Emphasize that ART is a set of brief sessions that are scripted — between one and five sessions. Reassure them that there is no homework — that the sessions are a complete experience of therapy, and the work is done through the assessment work by you (the therapist), and then the session work through scripting.

Remind your client about how the body remembers. Expand on that if they require you to. Tell them ART is ground-breaking because they, the client, will be aware of their body as their first step to interpreting somatic memory.

Share that within the sessions, the client will participate in image re-scripting. This is where the client imagines a new, positive way to remember the experience while being led by you to engage in the eye movements described earlier. With this, the original negative images are "replaced."

Emphasize that what ART practitioners find is that at the end of each session, the history of the original memory or event remains intact, but the client reports that sensory aspects of the memory have changed, and corresponding symptoms of the trauma (anxiety and panic attacks) are eliminated.

Share Laney Rosenzweig's words that, in ART we say:

> Keep the knowledge and lose the pain.

and

> Less gab and more grab.

and

> When in doubt, process out.

Being able to explain ART means coming up with what works for you and your client in the circumstances and environment you find yourself in. Lead from your strengths, and don't hesitate to return to your notes between sessions.

Share that ART is a paradigm shift in practice because we move the trauma first so the brain has space to learn skills and use tools because a part of it is freed up. Acknowledge to your client that this is a lot of information to take in, and that you will be leading them through the scripts that are used by, and are exclusive to, all ART therapists.

Ultimately, you want to demystify the process of treating trauma. Be at ease when you explain there are no secrets, that the therapy is linear, peer-reviewed, and proven. Reassure your client that there is no hidden agenda, and that they are safe.

LANGUAGE, FRAMING, REFRAMING

Ensure the overall message remains as one of comprehensive healing. You can master that by creating anticipation, and fostering curiosity.

Reframe almost everything as being helpful toward the goal of healing by refocussing attention on healing. Reframing can be used to manage resistance as it changes meaning into a symptom. Since symptoms can be dealt with, the reframing can later change how a client sees their whole life.

Normalize the client's story. Whatever the client brings, normalize all of their experiences and feelings. It is essential for them to know that they — and their family — are not alone.

Assure the client that they have all the internal resources to deal with the situation. As you work with them, use past-tense language, where appropriate, to refer to symptoms. This distancing will allow the client to establish a new definition of themselves — to see that old self in the past.

Build hope and connection through confident language when speaking about the therapy itself.

Utilize relevant stories that reflect the client's life story. Being told or telling a story that bridges to the therapeutic themes is a powerful communication tool, especially when positive and celebratory language is used.

Provide clear and predictable phases of work. When the therapy is described with specific, clear and finite stages, clients can feel a palpable excitement as positive change is within reach. When this happens, conscious and unconscious resources are mobilized quickly. Clients are better served when there is core targeting. Establish and share a developmental baseline, re-assessment, and fine-tuning with predictable progress and outcomes. It's essential the client sees that the therapy has an ending.

We can serve more effectively, and have greater outcomes to the therapy we provide, if we explain that therapy to a client as well as deliver it. You are an expert in your practice; your understanding is based on your profession, training, your previous education, the type of clinical practice you have, and your experiences in life overall. They will all shape your delivery of the explanation you give.

In addition to explaining ART, you may choose to, or not to, tell your whole professional story to your client — time or circumstance may not allow or be appropriate, but do not underestimate the value of healthy sharing. Your call to become a healer may be comprised of myriad academic and spiritual experiences, or one single magnetic message from which you could not turn away. You know, too, that the breakthroughs you've experienced with clients are explainable through science, timing and circumstance, and your guiding hand. We cannot move away from our therapeutic power, and we must remind our clients of their power too — their potential to heal.

QUESTIONS

What are some key elements of ART you want to be sure to explain to your clients?

Think of some relevant stories from your personal or therapeutic experience to integrate into your explanations of ART and make note of them here.

REFLECTIVE NOTES

CHAPTER 14
THE CONSULTATION CONVERSATION

Hello, I understand you were referred by your doctor. I'm so glad you could come. I'd like to spend an hour with you so that you can then be in a position to make the decision as to whether you want to do the work, and want to do the work with me.

~Short banter~

So, what was it like coming here? Traveling here today? And, if you've seen other therapists before, what's that been like?

~Client response~

Yeah, it can be hard. You probably have lots of questions. If you don't mind, though, I'll go first and share a bit about me and my background, then we can talk about why you've come to see me, and we can talk about trauma — I want to talk about trauma because I want to explain how I work and how I might be helpful. Then, I'll speak about Accelerated Resolution Therapy, or ART.

How does that sound?

~Client agrees~

Awesome. Let's go then. I'm a clinical social worker by profession — in the field for about thirty-eight years. I come from a trauma informed lens of practice — this means I always look at the root cause of a person's symptoms. There are those things we call symptoms, like anxiety, addiction, eating disorders… and they show up from root causes. There is trauma and then there are symptoms.

A million years ago, as a child welfare investigator, I was a first responder.

(I like to share this because so often I'm working with first responders as clients — I want them to know I was on the front lines too.)

The average time spent in the position of child welfare investigator is two years. I was in that position for seven. I had time to develop a lot of insight into situations — instead of looking at what was wrong with parents, I sought to understand them. I looked beyond the symptoms into the root causes of their issues.

What I discovered back then — way back then — is that people could do pretty amazing work if they would tell me what was going on — if they could give me a bit of their history so that I had more compassion for the situation. When that happened, we'd always work better together. In other words, I was looking for the root of the issues so as to not become reactive by *reacting* to the current situation.

I've had a private practice for more than thirty years and, back in the day, before operational stress injury was recognized as such, I'd get a call from someone saying, “Hey, Colleen, I heard you are doing some interesting therapy work that is different… can I come see you?”

So, I’ve worked with first responders for a long time and I’ve done a lot of expert course work. People have self-referred, others have been sent to me. My journey includes being the director at a hospice agency, a manager at a family services organization with a team of twenty-three and nine active programs, and teaching at the University of Calgary seven years, and many more years working directly with people on the subject of a trauma-informed lens. I’ve also spoken and presented overseas. A dozen or so years ago, I was invited to work with soldiers returning from Afghanistan.

Now, that was long, but please tell me, what’s going on right now as you listen to me?

~Client response~

That’s interesting. I hear that you’re feeling more comfortable, and you’re wondering what trauma is. I’m going to want to hear your story so that there can be some interweaving of our narratives, but let me take care of the trauma explanation first, okay?

Trauma is defined as any potential life-threatening event — physically, emotionally, sexually, spiritually, or psychologically. It’s important to know that trauma is individually based. What you might find traumatic may be different from what I do.

What happens when someone has a trauma, when the brain is not able to process that traumatic event, is that the event gets stuck in our frontal cortex.

When we go to sleep we typically go through the rapid-eye-movement, or REM, stage. This is when we can visibly notice movements under someone's eyelids. That eye movement is the body's natural way of processing the day-to-day stressors. It's a filter to reset ourselves to a good-to-go position.

For those who have trouble sleeping and/or cannot get to the level of deep-deep sleep, the brain has difficulty processing the trauma. There is no opportunity to apply that filter and reset.

How is your sleep?

~Client input~

I hear you. That certainly sounds like you're not sleeping as you used to. What's important to understand is that when your brain can't process out the trauma event, then that trauma remains present — and that means it is there to respond to triggers.

You're nodding. Ask me questions at any time — just jump in. I can see you understand that by the trauma not being processed out that it remains in your frontal cortex — in your head — and so you can become triggered by other events which then cause you to respond as if you are experiencing the trauma again.

The thing is, this is because of the amygdala. The amygdala has two parts, but for now I want to focus on it as one. Located at the base of the brainstem, its job — its only job — is to scan the environment for danger.

When it senses danger — and it does, often — then we are introduced to a fight, flight, or freeze response. We've all see this in creatures — all living creatures have this.

Whether we battle (fight), run away (flight), or stop everything (freeze) in response to a trigger, it is done through our senses: what we hear, smell, taste, see, and touch. When we are triggered, our body releases adrenaline. Our breathing becomes shallow, our heartbeat increases.

Did you experience that when you came to see me today?

~Client response~

Yes, that's common. It's called hyper-arousal. That's when we become super-aware of what's going on around us. We get jittery, even a bit suspicious, and are easily startled.

There is also something called hypo-arousal — that is when we numb out. We can feel our muscles get tight, and even get that deer-in-the-headlights feel.

I can see you're nodding; you understand the two concepts. Maybe you've experienced them. What I want to talk about now is the window of tolerance.

When someone cuts me off in traffic, my amygdala says "Hey! That guy cut me off." And my stress rises quickly. Then it comes down quickly because I'm thinking of something else: my mind goes to the shopping I am going to do, the meal I'll cook later. My stress was around zero… but it shot up quickly, even near ten. Then it went back to zero fairly fast. I just carried on driving.

But, for someone with PTSD, the stress — hyper-arousal — has not been at zero for a while. They are probably around five all the time. It is their normal to be set at five and not zero. Their starting point is a heightened state of arousal. It doesn't take long to get from five to ten. It is challenging to come down from ten once they are there.

Keeping that in mind, I'll later explain a concept called window of tolerance, and tools to use to stay in a safe range. I've got a lot more to share with you but, for now, can you tell me why you think therapy could help you?

~Client response~

It sounds like what you just told me has been a problem for years... that you did get a little relief at times, like when you said you did some cognitive behavioural therapy with a previous therapist. Seems like you've seen quite a few people in the past — and you've been feeling like all you do is talk about the traumatic event when you go to therapy.

Even bringing it up now, in a new situation, will be somewhat stressful, even though you may be hoping there will be relief.

~Client response~

Thanks for confirming that. Now, remember that trauma-informed lens I spoke of — me looking at the root cause of a person's symptoms? This way, this trauma-informed care allows me to focus on the root of the trauma.

Trauma work has to be evidence based. There are three different kinds of trauma work, and I'm trained in all of them. Basically, there's an exposure component a person has to go through — yes, go through the event — because the cortex is holding it, so it has to be put out there.

However, there are safe ways of doing this. I'm going to share with you the different kinds so you can understand how they work.

Remember, these are not ART — Accelerated Resolution Therapy — they are other therapies, but it's important you know about them.

The first trauma therapy I'll talk about is one called Prolonged Exposure, or EPT. Have you heard of it? It's been around since 1986, developed by Edna Foa. Just so you know, I am trained in EPT and have practiced it.

With EPT, a client goes through the event in a session, and then habituates it, to continue to go over it. The emotional response is recorded as the habituation continues.

Research on EPT says that it takes about fifteen sessions, and there's homework, to remove one event — clients are listening to a recording between sessions. A lot of therapists say that EPT is a difficult therapy to go through; people find the work hard to do and so they tend to drop out. It can be frustrating because the client will continue with the original belief of being broken or asking, "What's wrong? I can't get better."

I bet that sounds familiar.

~Client response~

The second trauma therapy is eye movement desensitization and reprocessing, or EMDR, which was developed in 1987 by Dr. Francine Shapiro. I trained under her in New York, in 1992. What I can tell you about EMDR is that it is similar to REM sleep, and is a non-talkative therapy.

The part of the brain that EMDR accesses is the frontal cortex. The therapy works with negative thoughts about the self because that's what gets stuck after trauma. When we've experienced trauma, we see the world and ourselves differently than pre-trauma. In this therapy, the protocol involves more free association as we review the events; the therapists will not know what door will open for each client — the client doesn't either.

It takes about twelve EMDR sessions to remove one negative cognition but, again, it takes four or five days to come back together between sessions, and that can be overwhelming and make it difficult for someone to continue. As well, because the events that will come up are not in any chosen order, the person in therapy may not be dealing with what they had intended to — it's a bit like the way a jack in the box operates in terms of *what* pops up rather than *when*.

The third therapy is Accelerated Resolution Therapy, or ART, which was created by Laney Rosenzweig, a therapist in Connecticut. She began working on its development around 2008.

Of course, ART is what you're here for. It's my chosen modality. I'm trained and certified and in fact I train other therapists in ART too.

ART represents a breakthrough in trauma therapy. It works from the bottom up — what I mean by that is that it settles the amygdala first, so that, as more therapy follows, the client is more responsive than reactive. Basically, the first thing this therapy does is dial down the amygdala.

With ART we have to go through an exposure component because we have to move the memory of the trauma — not the symptoms of it.

Imagine a railway track with seven rail cars on it, all hooked together. Can you see it? Now, think about this: each of the cars represents a step in ART that we work on. I guide clients — I'll guide you — through each step.

I'll complete a thorough assessment, and through that we'll identify themes which we will then divide into scenes. You'll be well-informed and understand each step — each car of the complete train.

Note: Here you'll want to describe the steps to your client. Write the eight steps out in a language that your client will understand. I let clients know, if they notice something, to write it down and let me know. This way, we can work on it next time, as we process different events and put them into themes.

Now, if at any point, today or during any of our ART sessions and we're working on one theme or scene, you notice something from a different scene, write it down and let me know. This way, we can work on it next time, as we process different events.

One way to look at how we structure our sessions is that the themes we've identified are like a riverbed with large boulders representing trauma, and that in one session, we've moved one trauma.

Each session can take about ninety minutes — fifteen to say where you're at, sixty for processing, and then another fifteen to check out. Sometimes sessions can be shorter.

Change happens quickly with ART. Because of that it can feel strange, since you've carried so much for so long and then you have released it.

Though I will have information about you in the pre-assessment, I might get to know more about you. But the nature of ART is relatively faster than most therapies, and so you likely won't be seeing me as long as you might see a therapist who works in one or more of the other modalities.

But you will likely continue or begin other therapies to deal with issues that have stemmed from holding the trauma. The great thing is after ART, other clients report that they can truly begin participating in other self-help groups they belong to — like AA, or NA, or even the gym.

I expect this might be the same for you.

End of consultation

QUESTIONS

How would you modify the content of this consultation script to make it your own, so you feel comfortable using it with your clients?

What is not included in this script that you would want to be sure to include?

REFLECTIVE NOTES

SECTION IV: THE FUTURE WITH ART

CHAPTER 15
COME PASSION

Despite its early successes, at the time of this writing ART is still an emerging therapy for the treatment of PTSD and other psychiatric conditions. ART was developed by an experienced master's level practitioner in a private practice, not in a university research setting. It has not yet had as much research-based validation as the other exposure-based therapies such as Prolonged Exposure, EMDR, CPT.

Five clinical trials of ART in PTSD have been completed and published. The study sizes are large, the results of the trials, as you have seen, are impressive. But the results must be interpreted with caution. All the studies were completed by the same research team at the University of Florida and only one study used a control group. A larger higher quality randomized controlled trial with 280 participants, conducted by Kathleen Chard at the University of Cincinnati and the VA Medical Center, comparing ART to CPT, has been underway since 2017 and was slated for completion in 2022. This is an important study which will answer many questions about the scientific support for ART.

So, what do we do in the absence of completed research? As a clinician, the parts of ART are very familiar in trauma treatment, with imaginal exposure, image re-scripting, processing of the somatic memory of trauma and use of bilateral stimulation all making intuitive sense. These elements have a wide and supportive research base and have demonstrated clinical effectiveness in the treatment of trauma.

Our patients are asking for treatment with ART and receiving benefit. So, I think we should apply ART in the clinical world, learn more in its application, do no harm, and keep one eye on academia to see if their new work will further assist us and our patients.

And when those academic studies support the results I see every day in clinic, as I believe they will, then we need to speak up about ART. We need to become advocates. People in leadership positions, who have the power to change policy and procedure, often have good intentions. But good intentions are not enough. Advocacy is required to inform those well-intentioned leaders about Accelerated Resolution Therapy.

The system needs a shift in practice from stabilization and symptom management to a trauma-informed lens of practice in Canada. ART basic trainings are provided on a regular basis to serve those clients who are asking for ART (word of mouth; grassroots in larger clinical settings starting small clinical trials; education of management and peers).

And so, I'd like to leave you with a final story of the healing power of ART.

This is the story of a veteran. There was no PTSD diagnosis, but the client's anxiety was high, depression was severe, and now doctors had also diagnosed them with cancer.

Anger issues rendered them unable to speak about their cancer. They were disconnected from a family member, and most other relationships in their life had either deteriorated or they had found a way to sabotage them before they could begin. They were so fearful.

They constantly tested me as we began therapy. The kind of testing was familiar to me and will be to you too: like a two-year-old trying to figure out if it was going to be a secure enough environment for them to be in.

They attended on a regular basis to engage in therapy. They received treatment for the cancer in another facility. We dealt with many of their issues and their mental health improved.

Then, suddenly, the cancer went into remission. So shocked were they to have that news, that they made some decisions to do things that they hadn't been able to do because they'd been unable to connect with others. It was a chance for a do-over.

They wanted a trailer and to travel. They repaired some relationships.

Then several years later, I received a call at the clinic that my client was in palliative care at a local hospital. Would I come and see them?

Of course, I went. The healed person wanted me to witness their will. They wanted me to know the things they were leaving for others, and why. Such loving reasons. And then they asked me for a hug.

"I'm ready to go," they said.

I commended them on what they'd done since therapy. My eyes teared with their progress on the road to love.

They had a final couple of wishes: that their partner would receive their pension, and that they could return to their beloved beautiful home and die there. I advocated for this and worked with the chaplain and others, finally receiving permission to have them transported to their little house.

"I'll see you on the other side," they said to me when I left.

They arrived at the little home with its view of the mountains. And they died the next day.

This was a person who had been so disconnected that anger was their defence. They lived a life of fear. ART allowed them to heal. What I did before ART contributed to that. My client was then able to surrender and transition peacefully — and put in some amazing years in between.

When we can accept our death, that's when we can accept our life. Accepting our suffering brings us to the door to surrender.

You'll recall at the start of this book, I said that the human spirit seeks to live, but when that human spirit has suffered trauma, or more than one, it first needs to heal.

You are equipped with ART to change lives, to go to the root of trauma so that your clients can recover, restart, return to school or work, and regain quality of life. Your role is to help them whisper, "Come, passion," to embrace the living that their trauma has been keeping them from.

And so I say to you, "Come, passion." Let the healing begin.

SECTION V: RESOURCES

INTRODUCTION TO RESOURCES

Lists are essential in streamlining our personal and professional lives. Of course, we are more than our lists; our focus and dedication go beyond checking off items, yet it is those lists which help assist us to be fully prepared and engaged with our clients.

I use this list, which is categorized, to cover key aspects of my work with each client. Whether you use it as is, or modify it, my intention is that it brings clarity to your sessions and streamlines your work.

IN MY PRACTICE RELATING TO ART

- Am I up-to-date with the current literature on trauma, including information from WHO, SAMHSA, APA (and/or the appropriate psychological association of each country)?
- Am I aware of updates from DSM and ICD editions?
- Have I updated/developed skills in cultural competence?
- Have I kept up with communication within the organization to which I belong and understand their expectations of me?
- Have I been practicing self-care?

- Do I regularly check my inner-voice as to whether it is highly self-critical?
- Do I use language that honours the client and promotes strength and safety?
- Have I asked for feedback lately?

WITH EACH CASE (ME AND MY CLIENT)

Have I:

- Gathered all the files I need?
- Made the therapy space comfortable and welcoming?
- Shared professional information about me with the client?
- Shared information about the clinic, and the interdisciplinary team to which I belong?
- Talked about the goals of therapy?
- Spoken about the importance of completing assignments and attending therapy?
- Reassured my client that trauma processing will be done when they are ready?
- Covered confidentiality? Asked for and obtained informed consent?
- Checked for a letter from a physician or psychiatrist regarding current medication?
- Reviewed PTSD, anxiety, or depression symptoms?
- Reviewed daily-routine stressors, barriers to attending therapy, stabilization?
- Discussed normalized symptoms?
- Reminded myself how easy it is to get into a loop with clients' symptoms?
- Overviewed other therapies?
- Made sure the client understands their diagnosis?

- Explored the possibility of a spouse or other family member attending a session, if applicable?
- Have I shared Robert Scaer's piece on trauma?
- Honoured their courage of coming to clinic/therapy?
- Emphasized their strengths?
- Discussed mindfulness and/or breathing exercises to combat hypo/hyper-arousal?

EXPLAINING THE DELIVERY OF ART TO MY CLIENT

Have I covered:

- ART is a paradigm shift in practice because the trauma is moved first
- ART was accredited by SAMHSA
- there is a lot of information to take in
- client's current knowledge of ART
- the phrase: "Keep the knowledge and lose the pain."

Psychoeducation:

- Concepts of loss and grief
- Window of tolerance
- Avoidance
- Basics of the brain
- Treatment phases, session structures and expectations
- Attachment and attachment patterns
- The topic of "the body keeps score"
- The client's working model and addressing core beliefs neg/pos

Using a whiteboard or paper, write goals and perceptions:

- asking how they saw the world before the trauma

- asking how they want to see the world
- checking what their world is like now
- identifying common patterns of early life experiences
- discussing the impact of childhood abuse (physical, emotional, sexual abuse, domestic violence, etc.) and neglect in adulthood

Developmental Themogram:

- Explain how they provide the foundation for healing
- Identify themes and scenes
- Eye movements
- Attunement

1. ART ADULT CONSENT FORM

Accelerated Resolution Therapy (ART) methodology is a form of adaptive information processing which may help the brain unlock maladaptive material. It also appears that ART may avoid some of the long and difficult abreacted work often involved in the treatment of anxiety, panic attacks, post-traumatic stress symptoms (such as intrusive thoughts, nightmares, and flashbacks), dissociative disorders, depression, phobias, identity crisis, and other traumatic experiences.

I acknowledge I have also been specifically advised of the following:

1) Distressing unresolved memories may surface through the use of the ART procedure.

2) Some clients experience reactions during the treatment sessions that neither they nor the administering clinician may have anticipated, including, but not limited to, high levels of emotional or physical sensations. Distressing memories may seem to disappear, while more pleasant memories may take their place during ART. Therefore, you should check with an attorney if you need to recall events for a legal procedure. These negative memories have

been more normally processed and are stored in a location that no longer bothers the clients. Subsequent to the treatment session, the processing of the incidents and/or material may continue and dreams, memories, flashbacks, feelings, etc., may surface.

3) Those with limiting or special medical conditions (pregnancy, heart condition, ocular difficulties, etc.) should consult their medical professionals before participating in ART treatment. ART treatment may put you at risk due to the possibility of heightened emotional reaction from ART treatment. For some people, this method may result in sharper memory, for others, it may result in less precise memory following the treatment. If you are involved in a legal case and need to testify, please discuss this with your therapist.

Before commencing ART treatment, I considered all of the above and obtained whatever additional input and/or professional advice I deemed necessary or appropriate.

I understand that I may stop treatment at any time before or during any ART session and that more than one ART session is usually necessary in the treatment.

With my signature below, I hereby consent to receive ART treatment. My signature on the acknowledgement and consent is free from pressure or influence from any person or entity. I have thoroughly read material explaining ART and understand it.

(Place space for client name, signature, and date, and witness name, signature, and date.)

2. ART CHILD/MINOR CONSENT FORM

Name of Child: ___________________

Date of Birth: __________________

Name of parent seeking treatment for child: __________________

Name of parent not present: ______________

This is to verify that I, (name of legal guardian)

_________________________________, am the legal guardian of:

______________________________ (name of child for whom treatment is being sought) have read, acknowledge, and consent to the following.

Accelerated Resolution Therapy (ART) methodology is a form of adaptive information processing which may help the brain unlock maladaptive material. It also appears that art may avoid some of the long and difficult abreacted work often involved in the treatment of anxiety, panic attacks, post-traumatic stress symptoms (such as intrusive thoughts, nightmares, and flashbacks), dissociative disorders, depression, phobias, identity crisis and other traumatic experiences.

I have also been specifically advised of the following:

1) Distressing unresolved memories may surface through the use of the ART procedure.

2) Some clients experience reactions during the treatment sessions that neither they nor the administering clinician may have anticipated, including, but not limited to, high levels of emotional or physical sensations. Distressing memories may seem to disappear, while more pleasant memories may take their place during ART. Therefore, you should check with an attorney if you need to recall events for a legal procedure. These negative memories have been more normally processed and are stored in a location that no longer bothers the clients. Subsequent to the treatment session, the processing of the incidents and/or material may continue and dreams, memories, flashbacks, feelings, etc., may surface.

3) Those with limiting or special medical conditions (pregnancy, heart condition, ocular difficulties, etc.) should consult medical professionals before participating in ART treatment. ART treatment may put you at risk due to the possibility of heightened emotional reaction from ART treatment. For some, this method may result in sharper memory, for others, it may result in less precise memory following the treatment. If you are involved in a legal case and need to testify, please discuss this with your therapist.

Before commencing ART treatment, I considered all of the above and obtained whatever additional input and/or professional advice I deemed necessary or appropriate.

I understand that I may stop treatment at any time before or during any ART session and that more than one ART session is usually necessary in the treatment.

I hearby consent that the above named child may receive family therapy, individual therapy (ART Accelerated Resolution Therapy), from Colleen E. Clark MSW RSW (1990), Clinical Social Worker (00126)

My signature below indicates that I hereby consent to receive therapy. My signature on the acknowledgement and consent is free from pressure or influence from any person or entity. We have thoroughly read material explaining ART and understand it and have informed consent for ART; individual and family therapy.

Client Print Name: ________________________________

Signature of Legal Guardian: __________________________

Date: __________________________

ART Therapist Signature: ____________________________

Witness Signature: __________________________________

Date: __________________________

3. ART WORKSHEET

Client Name:______________________________

Session #____________

ART Scene:

____

____

List Emotions:

____

____

____

____

Pre-SUDS: ______________________________

Post-SUDS: ______________________________

____

____

Scene Match (if needed):

____

____

Director Scene:

____

____

Snapshots:

____

____

Future Trigger Times:

____

____

Any clinical notes (e.g. metaphors used)

____

____

4. ART THEMES

FIRST RESPONDERS

Sudden Deaths

1. Natural deaths
2. Suicide (types)
3. Collision (motor vehicle accident) deaths
4. Accidental death (falls, shootings, etc.)
5. Member/veteran/first responder deaths

Children

1. SIDS (sudden infant death syndrome)
2. Accidents
3. Murder

Abuse

1. Physical

2. Emotional/psychological
3. Sexual
4. Neglect
5. Ritual Abuse
6. Torture
7. Abduction

MEDICAL EXAMINER/RCMP OR POLICE/EMS/MILITARY

Organizational moral injury (mistrust, betrayal, anger, shame, guilt)

- Sexual
- Bullying
- Harassment
- Environmental
- Racism
- Gender

Specialized units

- GIS
- Traffic
- CIS (ident)
- Homicide
- Dog handlers
- Special operations (strikes, Olympics, security, protection detail)
- Hostage taking/negotiations
- Undercover work
- Domestics
- Sexual assaults
- Major crimes
- Terrorism

- Torture
- Natural disasters
- Court

Career/Joining/job impacts

- How many, where, duration
- Age when joined, motivation to join
- Experiences during training
- Interpersonal (family, retirement, moves, divorce, infidelity)
- Disciplinary issues or events
- Time away from family (deployments, courses, training exercises)
- Financial issues
- Type of discharge from organization

COMPLEX TRAUMA

Loss and Grief

- Traumatic grief
- Disenfranchised grief
- Complicated grief

Career

- Discharge type from organization
- Medical (emotional and physical disabilities, pain)

Homicidal and Suicidal Ideation

- Attempts: how, when, what happened, outcome

5. STRUCTURE FOR ART THERAPY SESSIONS

SESSION 1: RELATIONSHIP BUILDING

- Therapist background: education, experience, philosophy of practice
- Information about the clinic, interdisciplinary team, consultation
- Treatment phases, session structures, expectations
- Reassure trauma processing will be done when client is ready
- Possibility of spouse joining next session
- CROMIS report, a tool to gauge how you are doing
- PCL-5, GAD, PHQ-9
- Establish if client has completed SES, if not, initiate series
- Review PTSD, anxiety, depression symptoms with client
- Normalize symptoms
- Honour courage to come to clinic
- Read article by Dr. Robert Scaer: "Healing Trauma and the Power of the Human Spirit"

Avoidance and its role in maintaining PTSD symptoms

- When intrusive thoughts or emotions are unbearable, client may naturally attempt to escape or avoid them
- This may work short term, but not long term
- Some forms of avoidance may lead to comorbid problems
- Maintaining symptom of PTSD-memory processing, e.g., substance use, keeping busy, missing therapy, not completing homework
- What does the client avoid
- Reiterate therapist/client role is addressing avoidance
- Importance of completing assignments and attending therapy
- Review daily routine-stressors, barriers to attending therapy, stabilization

SESSION 2: TRAUMA AND THE BRAIN

Emotions

- Threat generates naturally intense emotions is response to threat, loss
- Emotions provide us with important information about how to respond in a situation
- Primary vs. secondary emotions

The Brain

- Amygdala alarm centre, purpose is to keep us safe
- Danger detected? Amygdala activates emotions (fear or anger), sends neurotransmitters to the brain stem
- Initiates fight (anger), flight (anxiety, panic attack), or freeze response (tonic immobility, dissociation, example of a mouse playing dead)

- Triggered through the senses — ask for client's response
- Unnecessary functions are turned off-prefrontal cortex, is suppressed, digestion, etc.
- Circular relationship between prefrontal cortex and amygdala
- Under normal circumstances, prefrontal cortex is able to detect when danger is over and sends message to amygdala to stop the fight-flight response, stop neurotransmitters to brain stem
- Prefrontal cortex comes back online
- In PTSD, the prefrontal cortex shuts off too much, there is no message to stop amygdala to stop high response
- Vagus nerve: activates parasympathetic system. Deep breathing, progressive muscle relaxation, slow heart rate
- Window of tolerance

Role of Therapy

- Talking about trauma, labelling emotions, and keeping frontal cortex active helps bring the prefrontal cortex back online
- Therapy goal is to engage the rational part of the brain-awareness, mindfulness
- Increase window of tolerance: hyper-arousal vs. hypo-arousal
- Skills to expand window of tolerance include deep breathing, identifying triggers, mindfulness (practice in session)
- Introduce evidence-based trauma treatments (PE, EMDR, ART)

SESSION 3: PROFESSIONAL/WORK CULTURE

- Explore the client's experience in the workplace
- Why and how they joined
- Was training like a brotherhood, or membership, or other
- Hierarchy, values of the organization

- Intensity of exposure, isolation, numbness, and when they noticed changes, in perception of self, others, and the world
- Moral distress, shame, guilt

SESSION 4: CBT

- Client's values and beliefs before joining the organization
- Values and beliefs now (safety, the world, self esteem)
- What would the client like their values to be
- How would the client like to see the world
- Normalize
- Write/record the above, use to set goals and for later review
- Encourage client to take a photo if interested

SESSION 5: DEVELOPMENTAL THEMOGRAM

- Share M. Kitchur article
- Attunement in therapeutic relationship reparative (therapist flexible, sensitive, nurturing)
- Facilitate developmental catch-up: normalize client experiences, cultivate positive expectancy, recovery if possible, curiosity
- Resolve developmental condition that perpetuates the problem
- Use language that strengthen ego, impute resourcefulness and honour the person, hopefulness in recovery, assures safety

GRATITUDE

When certain individuals align with time to provide the exact lessons, input, and assistance, then that which is meant to be... becomes.

THE TRINITY

Dr. Stephen Boucher, my college friend and brilliant psychiatrist, has been right beside me from the beginning, envisioning our body of work to demystify trauma and complex trauma.

Stephen, you always come from a place of hope and inspiration and support. Brilliant, warm, and client centred, your generosity in gifting hours of analysis and questions has helped me build a magnificent therapeutic model that will live on. Your wisdom has benefited many. You validated my experience as a therapist and educator, and you blessed my calling.

Dr. Kevin Kip has held the vision of my being a trainer and presenter all through our association—and extended it to this book.

Kevin, you are a passionate individual whose research skills are second to none, critical thinking spot on, and your ability to analyze and bring new energy to projects is incredible.

Laney Rosenzweig, creator of Accelerated Resolution Therapy, is a developer and creator extraordinaire.

Laney, without your vision, your tenacity, and perseverance in bringing ART to the world, thousands of people would not know the healing that

ART provides, nor would this book have happened, nor would what follows this book in its future collaborative power take place.

Laney, you are boldly brilliant, beautifully eccentric, practicality personified, and no nonsense. I love how you keep things simple. Your brand of creativity is phenomenal. Thank you for creating the Rosenzweig Center for Rapid Recovery.

THE INVESTED AND THOUGHTFUL

Judy Fryer, business manager for RCRR, took on a supportive role in my development as the trainer for Canada. Her encouragement—from both professional and operational perspectives—kickstarted my own acumen; she could make a business model out of anything.

Judy, however you flow your spirit through the ether, may you know how treasured you were here in human form on this earth.

Robin Pickett, gifted administrator, fantastic multitasker, possessor of the most organized memory, she keeps the RCRR ship afloat. Robin, I deeply appreciate you always being accessible, supportive, and friendly.

Marney Riendeau, BSCN, RN, whose passion and innovation regarding managing military and RCMP provided the gateway for the first ART pilot project in Canada. Marney, I am forever indebted to you, for without your vision and support, ART would not be where it is in Canada.

The University of Calgary Faculty of Social Work: thank you for providing ongoing opportunities — for years — to be a sessional in delivering education for grads who then work in the field of mental health.

You facilitated my passion to teach and always treated me with great respect. It is a double pleasure to now train some of those graduates in ART.

The Profession of Social Workers:

I'm proud to share your values. Forty years ago, listening to the code of ethics, and being acknowledged in a classroom, was overwhelming and made me feel like I was home.

Agencies:

I'd like to pay tribute to a collective — dozens — of agencies from child protection services to hospices whose missions filled me with hope, and whose staff warmed me with pride and joy.

In a list of thank yous for a book about trauma, there is a necessity to thank each client — past, present, and future — for their vulnerability and their trust. It is here, on pages like this, and in outcomes provided by ART, that they can be reminded of their contribution to the whole, and acknowledged for their courage to heal.

SHAMANS:

I am profoundly grateful to those medicine men and women — natural healers — who exist on this earth. Their peaceful teaching and intuitive souls will always move us toward peace.

MOTHER EARTH:

To the collective that is every animal, human, plant, mountain, desert, ocean, river — she who has been segmented into nations, oceans, species, and emotions: I am forever grateful for your power, one that has pulled me as a golden thread through your tapestry.

Marie Beswick-Arthur, creative writing partner and editor, we've joked that you're the Raven to my White Owl. Black and White. Yin and Yang. Perhaps, Ink and Paper.

We knew each other before we knew each other — that can be the only reason you were able to understand the words of my heart. Thank you for your gift. May the world celebrate our partnership; even better, may the people of the world experience such an incredible relationship.

TO YOU

To those I have trained or influenced so far, and those I know only through the spirit of the healing profession, thank you for taking the words in this book, adding your own, and completing a truth collaboration. I'm indebted to you all for taking the torch and reconciling all beings in the world.

SURRENDER

I come to you oh God to surrender
Surrender all my fears, doubts, and questions
Of failing and not deserving.

I surrender
to you in overwhelming love

I surrender
that which is beyond trusting of the journey

I surrender
to you my God, my creator of everything

I surrender
that which is beyond my giving to self and others
as it holds a sense of reserve and control

I surrender
to and with your wisdom of giving me my purpose

I surrender
to your blessings for my joy

I surrender
to your peace and inter-connectedness to the whole

I surrender
to time and space

I surrender
to the now, the moment of everything

I surrender
to abundance, whatever that looks like

I surrender
to self through surrender to you as I am one with you

I surrender
to this journey, beyond the human form to where
soul dances and directs my life

I surrender
to love, pure love of self and others.

I surrender
in my role as healer as I stand today in the mountains

I surrender
for and to your guidance where my energy radiates freedom
now and forever

I surrender
no longer prisoner to old beliefs and messages of not being good
enough

I surrender
to and with your purest power and good for me

I surrender
to receive your blessings now, ready to be whole

I surrender
to you, my God, my father, my mother, my friend, my creator
in all eternity

Come bless me now and forever.

(Clark/1999)

About the Author

Colleen E. Clark, MSW, RCSW, BCETS, BCBT, BCFT, BCSA, and author, became a social worker in 1985, a clinical social worker in 1992, and has been in clinical private practice since 1994. She brings an inherent wisdom and depth of healing for the children, youth, teens, adults, couples and families she has had the honour to work with on their journey through healing to wholeness. Ms. Clark brought ART to Canada in 2014, and has since trained more than 1200 therapists from coast to coast to coast. She is a Master ART Practitioner, Clinical ART Specialist, ACSW Clinical Supervisor, RCRR

Lead Certified ART Trainer Canada. She is a diplomat with the American Academy of Experts in Traumatic Stress, is board certified in bereavement trauma and sexual abuse trauma, has presented her work nationally and internationally, and has been a sessional instructor at the University of Calgary in the Faculty of Social Work.

colleeneclarkconsulting.com

Contact Colleen if you're interested in receiving consultation or training from Colleen on her model.

BIBLIOGRAPHY

Blosnich, John R., Melissa E. Dichter, Catherine Cerulli, Sonja V. Batten, and Robert M. Bossarte. "Disparities in Adverse Childhood Experiences among Individuals with a History of Military Service." *JAMA Psychiatry* 71, no. 9 (September 1, 2014): 1041. https://doi.org/10.1001/jamapsychiatry.2014.724

Carlier, Ingrid V.E., Berthold P.R. Gersons, Regina D. Lamberts. "The Dimensionality of Trauma: A Multidimensional Scaling Comparison of Police Officers with and without Post-traumatic Stress Disorder." *Psychiatry Research* 97, no. 1 (December 2000): 29–39. https://web.archive.org/web/20230308192648/https://www.sciencedirect.com/science/article/abs/pii/S0165178100002110?via%3Dihub

Cloitre, Marylene, Lisa R. Cohen, Hyemee Han, Karestan C. Koenen. "Skills Training in Affective and Interpersonal Regulation Followed by Exposure: A Phase-Based Treatment for PTSD Related to Childhood Abuse." *Journal of Consulting and Clinical Psychology* 70, no. 5 (2002): 1067–74. https://web.archive.org/web/20230308234054/https://psycnet.apa.org/doiLanding?doi=10.1037/0022-006X.70.5.1067

———. Stephanie Cherry, Weijin Gan, Christie L. Jackson, Kate Nooner, Eva Petkova, K. Chase Stovall-McClough, Patty Zorbas. "Treatment for PTSD Related to Childhood Abuse: A Randomized Controlled Trial." *American Journal of Psychiatry* 167, no. 8 (August 2010): 915–24. /web/20230315213748/https://psychiatryonline.org/doi/abs/10.1176/appi.ajp.2010.09081247

———. Courtois, C.A., R. Carapezza, A. Charuvastra, B.L. Green, B.C. Stolbach. "Treatment of Complex PTSD: Results of the ISTSS Expert Clinician Survey on Best Practices." Journal of traumatic stress. U.S. National Library of Medicine. Accessed March 15, 2023. https://web.archive.org/web/20230316211929/https://pubmed.ncbi.nlm.nih.gov/22147449/

De Jongh, A., Edna B. Foa, Christopher W. Lee, Candice M. Monson, Patricia A. Resick, Agnes van Minnen, Lori A. Zoellner, et al. "Critical Analysis of the Current Treatment Guidelines for Complex PTSD in Adults." *Depression and Anxiety* 33, no. 5 (February 3, 2016): 359–69. https://web.archive.org/web/20230308195244/https://onlinelibrary.wiley.com/doi/10.1002/da.22469

———. *Practice Guidelines and Treatment of Complex PTSD* (Amsterdam, Netherlands: Psychotrauma Expertise Centrum, 2017).

Diagnostic and Statistical Manual of Mental Disorders: DSM-IV-TR. 4th Ed., Text Revision. Washington, DC: APA, 2000.

Diagnostic and Statistical Manual of Mental Disorders: DSM-5-TR. Washington, DC: American Psychiatric Association Publishing, 2022.

Felitti, V.J., R.F. Anda, V. Edwards , M.P. Koss, J.S. Marks, D. Nordenberg, D.F. Williamson, A. M. Spitz. "Relationship of Childhood Abuse and Household Dysfunction to Many of the

Leading Causes of Death in Adults. the Adverse Childhood Experiences (ACE) Study." American journal of preventive medicine. U.S. National Library of Medicine.

Finnegan, Alan, D. Hernandez, C. Hynes, K. Kip, S. McGhee, L. Rosenzweig, M. Thomas. "Accelerated Resolution Therapy: An Innovative Mental Health Intervention to Treat Post-Traumatic Stress Disorder." *Journal of the Royal Army Medical Corps* 162, no. 2 (July 3, 2015): 90–97.

Frangou, Christina. "For a Yazidi Refugee in Canada, the Trauma of ISIS Triggers Rare, Terrifying Seizures." *The Globe and Mail.* December 3, 2018. https://web.archive.org/web/20230316213048/https://www.theglobeandmail.-com/canada/article-for-a-yazidi-refugee-in-canada-the-trauma-of-isis-triggers-rare/

Germer, Christopher K. *The Mindful Path to Self-Compassion: Freeing Yourself from Destructive Thoughts and Emotions.* New York: Guilford Press, 2009.

Gill Rossiter, Alicia, Rita F. D' Aoust, Kevin E. Kip, Mireya Martin, Michaela R. Shafer. "Accelerated Resolution Therapy for Women Veterans Experiencing Military Sexual Trauma Related Post-Traumatic Stress Disorder." *Annals of Psychiatry and Mental Health* 5, no. 4 (2017): 1108.

Herman, Judith Lewis. "Complex PTSD: A Syndrome in Survivors of Prolonged and Repeated Trauma." *Journal of Traumatic Stress* 5, no. 3 (July 1992): 377–91. https://web.archive.org/web/20230308193705/https://doi.org/10.1002/jts.2490050305

Hernandez, Diego F., Mary Byrne, Lisseth Calvio, Wendi Waits. "Practice Comparisons between Accelerated Resolution Therapy, Eye Movement Desensitization and Reprocessing and Cognitive Processing Therapy with Case Examples." *Nurse Education Today* 47 (December 2016): 74–80. https://web.archive.org/web/20230308193932/https://doi.org/10.1016/j.nedt.2016.05.010

Hoge, Charles W. "Interventions for War-Related Post-traumatic Stress Disorder." *JAMA* 306, no. 5 (August 3, 2011). https://doi.org/10.1001/jama.2011.1096.

Institute of Medicine (US). Committee on Treatment of Alcohol Problems. "Broadening the Base of Treatment for Alcohol Problems." The National Academies Press.

Institute of Medicine. 2012. *Treatment for Post-traumatic Stress Disorder in Military and Veteran Populations: Initial Assessment.* Washington, DC: The National Academies Press. https://doi.org/10.17226/13364.

Kessler, Ronald C., Patricia Berglund, Olga Demler, Robert Jin, Kathleen R. Merikangas, and Ellen E. Walters. "Lifetime Prevalence and Age-of-Onset Distributions of DSM-IV Disorders in the National Comorbidity Survey Replication." *Archives of General Psychiatry* 62, no. 6 (June 1, 2005): 593. https://web.archive.org/web/20230308195731/https://jamanetwork.-com/journals/jamapsychiatry/fullarticle/208678

Kimerling, Rachel, Ruth C. Cronkite, Susan M. Frayne, Tyson H. Holmes, Joanne Pavao, Mark W. Smith, Amy E. Street. "Military-Related Sexual Trauma among Veterans Health Administration Patients Returning from Afghanistan and Iraq." *American Journal of Public Health* 100, no. 8 (August 2010): 1409–12. https://ajph.aphapublication-s.org/doi/full/10.2105/AJPH.2009.171793

Kip, Kevin E., Laney Rosenzweig, Diego F. Hernandez, Amy Shuman, David M. Diamond, Sue

Ann Girling, Kelly L. Sullivan, et al. "Accelerated Resolution Therapy for Treatment of Pain Secondary to Symptoms of Combat-Related Posttraumatic Stress Disorder." *European Journal of Psychotraumatology* 5, no. 1 (June 7, 2014). https://web.archive.org/web/20230216054656/https:/www.tandfonline.com/doi/full/10.3402/ejpt.v5.24066#

———. Diego F. Hernandez, Amy Shuman, Ann Witt, David M. Diamond, Sheryl Davis, Ryan Kip, et al. "Comparison of Accelerated Resolution Therapy (ART) for Treatment of Symptoms of PTSD and Sexual Trauma between Civilian and Military Adults." *Military Medicine* 180, no. 9 (September 2015): 964–71. https://doi.org/10.7205/milmed-d-14-00307. https://web.archive.org/web/20230308203839/https://academic.oup.com/milmed/article/180/9/964/4160577

———. Kelly L. Sullivan, Cecile A. Lengacher, Laney Rosenzweig, Diego F. Hernandez, Rajendra Kadel, Frank A. Kozel, et al. "Brief Treatment of Co-Occurring Post-Traumatic Stress and Depressive Symptoms by Use of Accelerated Resolution Therapy®." *Frontiers in Psychiatry* 4 (2013). https://web.archive.org/web/20230308201506/https://doi.org/10.3390/bs2020115

———. David M. Diamond, Diego F. Hernandez, Laney Rosenzweig, Amy Shuman. "Case Report and Theoretical Description of Accelerated Resolution Therapy (ART) for Military-Related Post-Traumatic Stress Disorder." *Military Medicine* 179, no. 1 (January 2014): 31–37. https://web.archive.org/web/20230308202757/https://academic.oup.com/milmed/article/179/1/31/4160691

———. David M Diamond. "Clinical, Empirical, and Theoretical Rationale for Selection of Accelerated Resolution Therapy for Treatment of Post-Traumatic Stress Disorder in VA and DOD Facilities." *Military Medicine* 183, no. 9-10 (April 4, 2018). /web/20230315222201/https://pubmed.ncbi.nlm.nih.gov/29635395/

———. Alisha Abhayakumar, Barrett Cuttino, Rita F. D'Aoust, Sue Ann Girling, Diego F. Hernandez, Mary Kathryn Long, Paola Rojas, Laney Rosenzweig, Trudy Wittenberg. "Evaluation of Brief Treatment of Symptoms of Psychological Trauma among Veterans Residing in a Homeless Shelter by Use of Accelerated Resolution Therapy." *Nursing Outlook* 64, no. 5 (October 2016): 411–23.

———. Rita F. D'Aoust, Sue Ann Girling, Yolanda Harper, and Laney Rosenzweig, Cindy Tofthagen. "Pilot Study of Accelerated Resolution Therapy for Treatment of Chronic Refractory Neuropathic Pain." *Alternative and Complementary Therapies* 22, no. 6 (December 2016): 243–50. https://web.archive.org/web/20230308204934/https://doi.org/10.1089/act.2016.29082.kek

———. Diego F. Hernandez, Christopher J. Long, Laney Rosenzweig, Amy Shuman, Kelly L. Sullivan, James Taylor, et al. "Randomized Controlled Trial of Accelerated Resolution Therapy (ART) for Symptoms of Combat-Related Post-Traumatic Stress Disorder (PTSD)." *Military Medicine* 178, no. 12 (December 2013): 1298–1309. https://web.archive.org/web/20230308202116/https://academic.oup.com/milmed/article/178/12/1298/4267504

Kneff, Kristin. *Self-Compassion: The Proven Power of Being Kind to Yourself.* London: Yellow Kite (Hodder & Stoughton), 2021.

Korn, Deborah L., and Andrew M. Leeds. "Preliminary Evidence of Efficacy for EMDR Resource Development and Installation in the Stabilization Phase of Treatment of Complex Post-traumatic Stress Disorder." *Journal of Clinical Psychology* 58, no. 12 (2002): 1465–87.

Litz, Brett. T., E. Delaney, L. Lebowitz, S. Maguen, W. P. Nash, C. Silva, N. Stein. (2009). Moral injury and moral repair in war veterans: a preliminary model and intervention strategy. *Clinical Psychology Review, 29*(8), 695–706. https://doi.org/10.1016/j.cpr.2009.07.003

Lonergan, Michelle. "Cognitive Behavioral Therapy for PTSD: The Role of Complex PTSD on Treatment Outcome." *Journal of Aggression, Maltreatment & Trauma* 23, no. 5 (May 16, 2014): 494–512. https://web.archive.org/web/20230316180236/https://www.tandfonline.-com/doi/abs/10.1080/10926771.2014.904467

Mcleod, Saul. "Erik Erikson's 8 Stages of Psychosocial Development." Study Guides for Psychology Students - Simply Psychology, February 24, 2023. https://web.archive.org/web/20230308220508/https://simplypsychology.org/Erik-Erikson.html

Milliken, Charles S., Jennifer L. Auchterlonie, Charles W. Hoge. "Longitudinal Assessment of Mental Health Problems among Active and Reserve Component Soldiers Returning from the Iraq War." *JAMA* 298, no. 18 (November 14, 2007): 2141. https://web.archive.org/web/20230316180500/https://jamanetwork.com/journals/jama/fullarticle/209441

Najavits, Lisa M. "The Problem of Dropout from 'Gold Standard' PTSD Therapies." *F1000Prime Reports* 7 (April 2, 2015). https://web.archive.org/web/20230308221215/https://facultyopinions.com/prime/reports/m/7/43

Orsillo, Susan M., Jane A. Luterek, Jennifer Plumb, Christina Theodore-Oklota. "The Development and Psychometric Evaluation of the Emotional Reactivity and Numbing Scale." *Journal of Nervous & Mental Disease* 195, no. 10 (October 2007): 830–36. DOI: 10.1097/NMD.0b013e318156816f

Pflanz, Steven. "Occupational Stress and Psychiatric Illness in the Military: Investigation of the Relationship between Occupational Stress and Mental Illness among Military Mental Health Patients." *Military Medicine* 166, no. 6 (June 1, 2001): 457–62. https://web.archive.org/web/20230316182128/https://academic.oup.com/milmed/article/166/6/457/4819386

Porges, Stephen W. *The Polyvagal Theory: Neurophysiological Foundations of Emotions, Attachment, Communication, and Self-Regulation*. New York: Norton, 2011.

"Post-Traumatic Stress Disorder: Management: Guidance." NICE. Accessed March 15, 2023. https://web.archive.org/web/20230128210531/https://www.nice.org.uk/guidance/NG116

Prigerson, Holly G., Paul K. Maciejewski, Robert A. Rosencheck. "Combat Trauma: Trauma with Highest Risk of Delayed Onset and Unresolved Post-traumatic Stress Disorder Symptoms, Unemployment, and Abuse among Men." *The Journal of Nervous and Mental Disease* 189, no. 2 (February 2001): 99–108. https://web.archive.org/web/20230308222151/https://doi.org/10.1097/00005053-200102000-00005

Ramchand, Rajeev, Rachel M. Burns, Leah Barnes Caldarone, Benjamin R. Karney, Karen Chan Osilla, Terry L. Schell. "Disparate Prevalence Estimates of PTSD among Service Members Who Served in Iraq and Afghanistan: Possible Explanations." *Journal of Traumatic Stress* 23, no. 1 (February 2010): 59–68. https://web.archive.org/web/20230316183313/https://onlinelibrary.wiley.com/doi/10.1002/jts.20486

Resick, Patricia A., Michelle J. Bovin, Amber L. Calloway, Alexandra M. Dick, Matthew W. King, Karen S. Mitchell, Michael K. Suvak, Stephanie Y. Wells, Shannon Wiltsey Stirman, and Erika J. Wolf. "A Critical Evaluation of the Complex PTSD Literature: Implications for DSM-5." *Journal of Traumatic Stress* 25, no. 3 (June 2012): 241–51. https://web.archive.org/web/20230316183458/https://onlinelibrary.wiley.-com/doi/10.1002/jts.21699

Ritchie, Elspeth Cameron. *Post-traumatic Stress Disorder and Related Diseases in Combat Veterans*. Cham: Springer, 2015.

Rona, Roberto J., Howard Burdett, Samantha Bull, Nicola T. Fear, Neil Greenberg, Margaret Jones, Norman Jones, Simon Wessely. "Prevalence of PTSD and Other Mental Disorders in UK Service Personnel by Time since End of Deployment: A Meta-Analysis." *BMC Psychiatry* 16, no. 1 (September 22, 2016). https://web.archive.org/web/20230308230735/https://doi.org/10.1186/s12888-016-1038-8

Rothschild, Babette. *Revolutionizing Trauma Treatment: Stabilization, Safety, & Nervous System Balance.* New York, New York. W.W. Norton & Company, 2021.

Schottenbauer, Michele A., Diane B. Arnkoff, Carol R. Glass, Sheila Hafter Gray, Vanessa Tendick. "Nonresponse and Dropout Rates in Outcome Studies on PTSD: Review and Methodological Considerations." *Psychiatry: Interpersonal and Biological Processes* 71, no. 2 (June 2008): 134–68. https://web.archive.org/web/20230316203511/https://guilfordjournals.com/doi/10.1521/psyc.2008.71.2.134

Seal, Karen H., Daniel Bertenthal, Kristian S. Gima, Shira Maguen, Charles R. Marmar, Thomas J. Metzler. "Trends and Risk Factors for Mental Health Diagnoses among Iraq and Afghanistan Veterans Using Department of Veterans Affairs Health Care, 2002–2008." *American Journal of Public Health* 99, no. 9 (September 2009): 1651–58. https://web.archive.org/web/20230308231224/https://doi.org/10.2105/AJPH.2008.150284

Shapiro, Robin. *EMDR Solutions: Pathways to Healing.* New York: Norton, 2005.

Siegel, Daniel J. *The Developing Mind: How Relationships and the Brain Interact to Shape Who We Are*. New York: Guilford Press, 2015.

Shay, Jonathan. "Moral Injury." *Psychoanalytic Psychology* 31, no. 2 (April 2014): 182–91. https://web.archive.org/web/20230308231404/https://doi.org/10.1037/a0036090

Sugaya, Luisa, Carlos Blanco, Bridget F. Grant, Deborah S. Hasin, Keng-Han Lin, Mark Olfson. "Child Physical Abuse and Adult Mental Health: A National Study." *Journal of Traumatic Stress* 25, no. 4 (July 16, 2012): 384–92. https://web.archive.org/web/20230316203826/https://onlinelibrary.wiley.-com/doi/10.1002/jts.21719

Terr, Lenore C. "Childhood Traumas: An Outline and Overview." *FOCUS* 1, no. 3 (July 2003):

322–34. https://web.archive.org/web/20230316204627/https://focus.psychiatryonline.org/doi/full/10.1176/foc.1.3.322

Tuerk, Peter W., Ron Acierno, Clara E. Dismuke, Afsoon Eftekhari, Hugh Myrick, Sheila A. Rauch, Bethany Wangelin, Matthew Yoder. “Health Service Utilization before and after Evidence-Based Treatment for PTSD.” *Psychological Services* 10, no. 4 (2013): 401–9. https://web.archive.org/web/20230308232003/https://psycnet.apa.org/doiLanding?doi=10.1037/a0030549

van der Kolk, Bessel A., David Pelcovitz, Susan Roth, Joseph Spinazzola, Susanne Sunday. “Disorders of Extreme Stress: The Empirical Foundation of a Complex Adaptation to Trauma.” *Journal of Traumatic Stress* 18, no. 5 (2005): 389–99. https://web.archive.org/web/20230316205229/https://onlinelibrary.wiley.com/doi/10.1002/jts.20047

Van Voorhees, Elizabeth E., Jean C. Beckham, Mira Brancu, Patrick S. Calhoun, Eric A. Dedert, Jennifer Runnals. “Childhood Trauma Exposure in Iraq and Afghanistan War Era Veterans: Implications for Post-traumatic Stress Disorder Symptoms and Adult Functional Social Support.” *Child Abuse & Neglect* 36, no. 5 (May 2012): 423–32. https://web.archive.org/web/20230308232518/https://www.sciencedirect.com/science/article/abs/pii/S0145213412000798?via%3Dihub

Waits, Wendi, Megan Marumoto, and Jennifer Weaver. “Accelerated Resolution Therapy (ART): A Review and Research to Date.” *Current Psychiatry Reports* 19, no. 3 (March 2017). https://web.archive.org/web/20230308232737/https://link.springer.com/article/10.1007/s11920-017-0765-y

World Health Organization, 1992. *The ICD-10 Classification of Mental and Behavioural Disorders: Clinical Descriptions and Diagnostic Guidelines.*

Yehuda, Rachel. *Treating Trauma Survivors with PTSD, 1st Edition*. Washington, DC: American Psychiatric Association Publishing, 2002.

Zetterberg, Jenny. "Trauma and recovery: a literature study of Dr. Judith Herman’s research and treatment methodology." (2010).

www.ingramcontent.com/pod-product-compliance
Ingram Content Group UK Ltd.
Pitfield, Milton Keynes, MK11 3LW, UK
UKHW020203290926
15471UKWH00005B/1037

9 783988 323101